Narrative Fiction

What is a narrative? What is narrative fiction? How does it differ from other kinds of narrative? What features turn a discourse into a narrative text? Now widely acknowledged as one of the most significant volumes in its field, *Narrative Fiction* turns its attention to these and other questions.

In contrast to many other studies, *Narrative Fiction* is organized around issues – such as events, time, focalization, characterization, narration, the text and its reading – rather than individual theorists or approaches. Within this structure, Shlomith Rimmon-Kenan addresses key approaches to narrative fiction, including New Criticism, formalism, structuralism and phenomenology, but also offers views on the modifications to these theories. While presenting an analysis of the system governing all fictional narratives, whether in the form of novel, short story or narrative poem, she also suggests how individual narratives can be studied against the background of this general system. A broad range of literary examples illustrate key aspects of the study.

This edition is brought fully up-to-date with an invaluable new chapter, reflecting on recent developments in narratology. Readers are also directed to key recent works in the field. These additions to a classic text ensure that *Narrative Fiction* will remain the ideal starting point for anyone new to narrative theory.

Shlomith Rimmon-Kenan is Professor of English and Comparative Literature at the Hebrew University of Jerusalem. Her most recent publications include *A Glance Beyond Doubt: Narration, Representation, Subjectivity* (1996) and *Re-Reading Texts: Re-Thinking Critical Presuppositions* (edited, 1997). Her current project concerns the concept of narrative in different disciplines (psychoanalysis, historiography, legal studies and the medical humanities).

IN THE SAME SERIES

Shlomith
Rimmon-Kenan

Narrative Fiction

Contemporary Poetics

2nd edition

Routledge
Taylor & Francis Group

LONDON AND NEW YORK

First published 1983 by Methuen & Co. Ltd
Reprinted five times

Reprinted 1989, 1992, 1993, 1994, 1996, 1999 (twice), 2001
by Routledge
11 New Fetter Lane, London EC4P 4EE
29 West 35th Street, New York, NY 10001

This edition first published 2002

Reprinted 2003

Transferred to Digital Printing 2003

Routledge is an imprint of the Taylor & Francis Group

© 1983, 2002 Shlomith Rimmon-Kenan

Typeset in Joanna by RefineCatch Limited, Bungay, Suffolk
Printed and bound in Great Britain by
TJI Digital, Padstow, Cornwall

British Library Cataloguing in Publication Data
A catalogue record for this book is available from the British Library

Library of Congress Cataloging in Publication Data
A catalog record for this book has been requested

ISBN 0–415–28021–4 (Hbk)
ISBN 0–415–28022–2 (Pbk)

To Guy, who suffered

CONTENTS

GENERAL EDITOR'S PREFACE

No doubt a third General Editor's Preface to *New Accents* seems hard to justify. What is there left to say? Twenty-five years ago, the series began with a very clear purpose. Its major concern was the newly perplexed world of academic literary studies, where hectic monsters called 'Theory', 'Linguistics' and 'Politics' ranged. In particular, it aimed itself at those undergraduates or beginning postgraduate students who were either learning to come to terms with the new developments or were being sternly warned against them.

New Accents deliberately took sides. Thus the first Preface spoke darkly, in 1977, of 'a time of rapid and radical social change', of the 'erosion of the assumptions and presuppositions' central to the study of literature. 'Modes and categories inherited from the past' it announced, 'no longer seem to fit the reality experienced by a new generation'. The aim of each volume would be to 'encourage rather than resist the process of change' by combining nuts-and-bolts exposition of new ideas with clear and detailed explanation of related conceptual developments. If mystification (or downright demonisation) was the enemy, lucidity (with a nod to the compromises inevitably at stake there) became a friend. If a 'distinctive discourse of the future' beckoned, we wanted at least to be able to understand it.

With the apocalypse duly noted, the second Preface proceeded piously to fret over the nature of whatever rough beast might stagger portentously from the rubble. 'How can we recognise or deal with the new?', it complained, reporting nevertheless the dismaying advance of 'a host of barely respectable activities for which we have no reassuring names' and promising a programme of wary surveillance at 'the boundaries of the precedented and at the limit of the thinkable'. Its conclusion, 'the unthinkable, after all, is that which covertly shapes our thoughts' may rank as a truism. But in so far as it offered some sort of useable purchase on a world of crumbling certainties, it is not to be blushed for.

In the circumstances, any subsequent, and surely final, effort can only modestly look back, marvelling that the series is still here, and not unreasonably congratulating itself on having provided an initial outlet for what turned, over the years, into some of the distinctive voices and topics in literary studies. But the volumes now re-presented have more than a mere historical interest. As their authors indicate, the issues they raised are still potent, the arguments with which they engaged are still disturbing. In short, we weren't wrong. Academic study did change rapidly and radically to match, even to help to generate, wide-reaching social changes. A new set of discourses was developed to negotiate those upheavals. Nor has the process ceased. In our deliquescent world, what was unthinkable inside and outside the academy all those years ago now seems regularly to come to pass.

Whether the *New Accents* volumes provided adequate warning of, maps for, guides to, or nudges in the direction of this new terrain is scarcely for me to say. Perhaps our best achievement lay in cultivating the sense that it was there. The only justification for a reluctant third attempt at a Preface is the belief that it still is.

TERENCE HAWKES

ACKNOWLEDGEMENTS

This book was begun in collaboration with Moshe Ron who, unfortunately, had to withdraw in a fairly early stage. In addition to specific sections based on his contribution and acknowledged throughout the book, I am also grateful for his participation in planning the overall conception, for numerous stimulating discussions of the poetics of narrative fiction, and for his scrupulous and perceptive comments on a large part of the manuscript. Thanks are also due to Joseph Ewen, Ruth Ginsburg, Harai Golomb, Baruch Hochman, Benjamin Hrushovski, Joyce Miller and Myriam Saguy, whose help in clarifying my thinking on various issues was invaluable. Professor Terence Hawkes, the general editor of this series, has done much to improve the readability of my text. To Ruth and Natan Nevo I am indebted for constant encouragement in times of frustration. I also wish to thank Sylvia Farhi, in whom I found not only an excellent typist but also a wonderful person. Over the years I have been helped and challenged by students in various courses I have taught on the subject. To all of them I am grateful.

The author and publisher would like to thank Faber & Faber Ltd and Harcourt Brace Jovanovich, Inc. for permission to reproduce four lines from 'Little Gidding' in Four Quartets, copyright 1943 by T. S. Eliot; renewed 1971 by Esme Valerie Eliot.

S.R.-K.

1

INTRODUCTION

Newspaper reports, history books, novels, films, comic strips, pantomime, dance, gossip, psychoanalytic sessions are only some of the
narratives which permeate our lives. One species of narrative will be
the subject of this book: the species called 'narrative fiction',whether in
the form of novel, short story or narrative poem.

But what is a narrative? What makes the following limerick a
narrative?

> There was a young lady of Niger
> Who smiled as she rode on a tiger.
>> They returned from the ride
>> With the lady inside
> And the smile on the face of the tiger.

How can we differentiate between this limerick and the following
discourse?

> Roses are red
> Violets are blue
> Sugar is sweet
> And so are you.

Why isn't the latter a narrative?

And what is narrative fiction? How does it differ from other kinds of narrative? In what sense is a newspaper report, like 'yesterday a store in Oxford Street was burned out' a narrative but not narrative fiction? What are the features that turn a given discourse into a narrative text? What are the basic aspects of narrative fiction and how do they interact with each other? How does one make sense of a specific narrative text, and how can it be described to others?

These and other questions will be considered in some detail throughout this book. However, it is helpful to begin with working definitions of the key terms of the title, thus providing a framework for further deliberations.

Poetics is

> the systematic study of literature as literature. It deals with the question 'What is literature?' and with all possible questions developed from it, such as: What is art in language? What arc the forms and kinds of literature? What is the nature of one literary genre or trend? What is the system of a particular poet's 'art' or 'language'? How is a story made? What are the specific aspects of works of literature? How are they constituted? How do literary texts embody 'non-literary' phenomena? etc.
>
> (Hrushovski 1976b, p. xv)

By 'narrative fiction' I mean the narration of a succession of fictional events. Self-evident as this definition may seem, it nevertheless implies certain positions with regard to some basic issues in poetics. To begin with, the term *narration* suggests (1) a *communication* process in which the narrative as message is transmitted by addresser to addressee and (2) the *verbal* nature of the medium used to transmit the message. It is this that distinguishes narrative fiction from narratives in other media, such as film, dance, or pantomime.[1]

The definition further suggests how narrative fiction differs from other literary texts, such as lyrical poetry or expository prose. Unlike the latter, narrative fiction represents a *succession of events* (Tomashevsky 1965, p. 66. Orig. publ. in Russian 1925). At this early stage of our discussion, an *event* may be defined without great rigour as something that happens, something that can be summed up by a verb or a name of action (e.g. a ride − perhaps on a tiger). Although single-event narratives are theoretically (and perhaps also empirically) possible (see chapter 2), I speak of a *succession* of events in order to suggest that narratives usually consist of more than one. Thus the lady in the limerick first rides on a tiger, then returns in it.

Finally, the main interest of this book is in narratives of *fictional* events. This is why I shall not consider here nonfictional verbal narratives, like gossip, legal testimony, news reports, history books, autobiography, personal letters, etc. The fictional status of events is, I believe, a pragmatic issue. It is arguable that history books, news reports, autobiography are in some sense no less fictional than what is conventionally classified as such. In fact, some of the procedures used in the analysis of fiction may be applied to texts conventionally defined as 'non-fiction'. Nevertheless, since such texts will also have characteristics specific to them, they are beyond the scope of this book.

The foregoing definition of narrative fiction also gives rise to a classification of its basic aspects: the events, their verbal representation, and the act of telling or writing. In the spirit of Genette's distinction between 'histoire', 'récit' and 'narration' (1972, pp. 71−6), I shall label these aspects 'story', 'text' and 'narration' respectively.[2]

'Story' designates the narrated events, abstracted from their disposition in the text and reconstructed in their chronological order, together with the participants in these events.

Whereas 'story' is a succession of events, 'text' is a spoken or written discourse which undertakes their telling. Put more simply, the text is what we read. In it, the events do not necessarily appear in chronological order, the characteristics of the participants are dispersed throughout, and all the items of the narrative content are filtered through some prism or perspective ('focalizer').

Since the text is a spoken or written discourse, it implies someone who speaks or writes it. The act or process of production is the third aspect − 'narration'. Narration can be considered as both real and fictional. In the empirical world, the author is the agent responsible for the production of the narrative and for its communication. The empirical process of communication, however, is less relevant to the poetics of narrative fiction than its counterpart within the text. Within the text, communication involves a fictional narrator transmitting a narrative to a fictional narratee.

Of the three aspects of narrative fiction, the text is the only one directly available to the reader. It is through the text that he or she acquires knowledge of the story (its object) and of the narration (the process of its production). On the other hand, however, the narrative text is itself defined by these two other aspects: unless it told a story it would not be a narrative, and without being narrated or written it would not be a text. Indeed, story and narration may be seen as two metonymies of the text, the first evoking it through its narrative content, the second through its production.[3] The relations among the aspects will be emphasized throughout this study, and the aspects themselves will inform the division into chapters.

Thus far I have suggested preliminary answers to all but the last two questions set forth in the beginning of this introduction. These two questions differ from the others in that they concern the specificity of individual texts rather than characteristics common to all works of narrative fiction. Indeed, the copresence of these two types of question is indicative of the double purpose of this book. On the one hand, I wish to present a description of the system governing all fictional narratives. On the other hand, I hope to indicate a way in which individual narratives can be studied as unique realizations of the general system.

This double orientation calls for a mixture of theoretical considerations and illustrations from works of narrative fiction. Of course, some issues are more amenable to illustration while others necessitate a more abstract discussion. The distribution of examples will vary accordingly. For reasons of space and variety, I do not analyse any text in full but prefer a discussion of extracts from many texts, deriving from various periods and various national literatures. Some examples are repeated in different contexts. This is done not only for the sake of reinforcement but also in order to emphasize that textual segments are junctions of various compositional principles, not ready-made examples of any one principle to the exclusion of others (although a predominance of one is obviously possible). Analysis requires emphasis on the issue under consideration, but texts are richer than anything such an isolation of aspects can yield.

My presentation draws upon Anglo-American New Criticism, Russian Formalism, French Structuralism, the Tel-Aviv School of Poetics and the Phenomenology of Reading. However, the book is not structured according to 'schools' or individual theoreticians (as, for example, Hawkes 1977). Rather, it is organized around the *differentia specifica* of narrative fiction (e.g. events, time, narration). The predilection revealed here for certain approaches as well as the selection of specific aspects from each approach imply a personal stand on the various issues. Nor is this stand confined to tacit implication: on the contrary, it often manifests itself in explicit comments on and modifications of the theories which are brought together. Yet this book does not offer an original theory. Indeed the tension between an integration of existing theories and a presentation of a personal view is one of the inevitable frustrations of any attempt at a synthesis. Similarly, it was necessary to extract the relevant points from each theory without presenting the theory as a whole or following all of its implications. It is hoped that the reader will be encouraged to continue to explore this field, and by so doing to fill in some of these lacunae.

2

STORY: EVENTS[1]

THE QUESTION OF THE STORY'S AUTONOMY

Story was defined above as the narrated events and participants in abstraction from the text. As such, it is a part of a larger construct, referred to by some as the 'reconstructed' (or 'represented') world (or 'level') (e.g. Hrushovski 1976a, p. 7), i.e. the fictional 'reality' in which the characters of the story are supposed to be living and in which its events are supposed to take place. In fact, story is one axis within the larger construct: the axis of temporal organization. Since this is the axis whose predominance turns a world-representing text into a narrative text, I shall confine my discussion to it, leaving out the broader construct which is not specifically narrative.

Being an abstraction, a construct, the story is not directly available to the reader. Indeed, since the text is the only observable and object-like aspect of verbal narrative, it would seem to make sense to take it as the anchoring-point for any discussion of the other aspects – as I do in chapters 4, 5 and 6. What I believe is called for here is a defence of the decision to treat story in isolation in this and the next chapter.

Far from seeing story as raw, undifferentiated material, this study stresses its structured character, its being made of separable components, and hence having the potential of forming networks of internal relations. Such a view justifies attempts to disengage a form from the substance of the narrated content, a specific narrative form.[2] The theoretical possibility of abstracting story-form probably corresponds to the intuitive skill of users in processing stories: being able to re-tell them, to recognize variants of the same story, to identify the same story in another medium, and so on. It is this intuition that has led almost every narratologist following in Vladimir Propp's footsteps to formulate a claim that an immanent story structure, sometimes called 'narrativity', may be isolated at least for the sake of description. What Propp studied in his *Morphology of the Russian Folk-tale*, writes Bremond, was an 'autonomous layer of meaning'. He goes on:

> The subject of a tale may serve as an argument for a ballet, that of a novel may be carried over to the stage or to the screen, a movie may be told to those who have not seen it. It is words one reads, it is images one sees, it is gestures one deciphers, but through them it is a story one follows; and it may be the same story.
>
> (Bremond 1964, p. 4. Ron's translation)

A stronger stance is taken by Greimas, according to whom an acknowledgement of Bremond's point

> amounted to recognizing and accepting the necessity of a fundamental distinction between two levels of representation and analysis: an *apparent* level of narration, at which the manifestations of narration are subject to the specific exigencies of the linguistic substances through which they are expressed, and an *immanent level*, constituting a sort of common structural trunk, at which narrativity is situated and organized prior to its manifestations. A common semiotic level is thus distinct from the linguistic level and is logically prior to it, whatever the language chosen for manifestation.
>
> (Greimas 1977, p. 23. Orig. publ. in French 1969)[3]

What emerges from these statements (and one could add Prince 1973, p. 13) is that story is an abstraction from: (1) the specific style of the text in question (e.g. Henry James's late style, with its proliferation of subordinate clauses, or Faulkner's imitation of Southern dialect and rhythm, (2) the language in which the text is written (English, French, Hebrew) and (3) the medium or sign-system (words, cinematic shots, gestures). Starting with story, rather than with the text from which it is abstracted, the former may be grasped as transferable from medium to medium, from language to language, and within the same language.

This view can be opposed by the equally intuitive counter-conviction of many trained literary readers that literary works, not excluding their story aspect, 'lose something' in paraphrase or 'translation' (lose more than something, say, in their Hollywood version). In other words, stories – the claim is – are in some subtle ways style-, language-, and medium-dependent. This is forcefully stated by Todorov in an early work:

> Meaning does not exist before being articulated and perceived ... ; there do not exist two utterances of identical meaning if their articulation has followed a different course.
>
> (1967, p. 20. Ron's translation)

If accepted, such a view suggests some limits on the notion of translatability in general.[4] Indeed, readers with a fanatic attitude about the 'heresy of paraphrase' (an expression coined by Cleanth Brooks 1947) will have little use for the study of story as such.

Still, as with so-called natural language, users cannot produce or decipher stories without some (implicit) competence in respect of narrative structure, i.e. in something which survives paraphrase or 'translation'. This competence is acquired by extensive practice in reading and telling stories. We are faced here with the same epistemological dialectic which binds together any opposition of the virtual and the actual (such as 'langue' v. 'parole' in Saussure, 'competence' v. 'performance' in Chomsky. See Culler 1975, pp. 8–10; Hawkes 1977, pp. 21–2). In this predicament, the preliminary assumption that story-structure or narrativity is isolatable must be made at least as a working hypothesis. This, however, does not amount to granting any undisputed priority, whether logical or ontological, to story over text (if forced to decide, I would rather opt for the latter).

THE NOTION OF NARRATIVE GRAMMAR

Although story is transverbal, it is often claimed to be homologous (i.e. parallel in structure) to natural language and hence amenable to the type of analysis practised in linguistics. Such analysis frequently takes the form of the construction of narrative 'grammars', whether involving a direct application of linguistic methods and terms which in some sense become metaphorical, as in Todorov's *Grammaire du Décaméron* (1969), or a broader notion of 'grammar' as in Greimas's statement:

> The linguist, then, will not fail to take note that narrative structures present characteristics which are remarkably *recurrent*, and these recurrences allow for the recording of distinguishable *regularities*, and that they thus lead to the construction of a *narrative grammar*. In this case it is evident that he will utilize the concept of grammar in its most general and non-metaphorical sense, understanding such a grammar to consist in a limited number of principles of structural organization of narrative units, complete with rules for the combination and functioning of these units, leading to the production of narrative objects.
>
> (1971, p. 794)

In recent years, narrative grammar has become a highly specialized field, where every move requires more methodological considerations and more rigorous formalizations than I can deal with here.[5] Within this chapter it is impossible to construct a narrative grammar or even to offer an adequate survey of existing proposals for such a grammar. Only an eclectic and cursory presentation of a few main notions deriving from several models can be attempted here. However, I shall borrow from such grammars the concepts of deep and surface structure, using them as organizing principles for the rest of this chapter. In so doing, I shall include under these headings both issues which were explicitly raised within this framework and others which can now be seen to contribute to it, even though they were developed independently.

The notions of deep and surface structure come from 'transformational generative grammar', which undertakes to enumerate (characterize) the infinite set of sentences of a language by positing a finite number of deep-structure (phrase-structure) rules and a set of trans-formational rules which convert deep structures to surface structure. Whereas surface structure is the abstract formulation of the organiza-tion of the observable sentence, deep structure – with its simpler and more abstract form – lies beneath it and can only be retrieved through a backward retracing of the transformational process. Thus, the sen-tences 'The police killed the thief' and 'The thief was killed by the police' have different surface structures (subject + predicate + direct object v. subject + predicate + indirect object – to use traditional syntactic terminology). They also assign the same words to different structural positions, the thief being object in the first and subject in the second, the police being subject in the first and indirect object in the second. Nevertheless, the two sentences have the same deep structure, since the passive form is a *transformation* of the active. Conversely, a sentence like 'Flying planes can be dangerous' has one surface structure but two deep structures, depending on whether we take it to mean 'it can be dangerous (for someone) to fly planes' or 'planes which fly (as opposed to those that stand) can be dangerous'.

Theorists of narrative who are interested in how the infinite variety of stories may be generated from a limited number of basic structures often have recourse, like linguists, to the notions of deep and surface structure. Both surface and deep *narrative* structures underlie the surface and deep *linguistic* structures of the verbal narrative text:

> To the two linguistic levels
> 1 surface linguistic structures
> 2 deep linguistic structures
> two other narrative levels are added:
> 3 surface narrative structures
> 4 deep narrative structures.
>   (Greimas 1971, p. 797)

Whereas the surface structure of the story is syntagmatic, i.e. governed by temporal and causal principles, the deep structure is paradigmatic, based on static logical relations among the elements (see examples in the section below). This is why deep structures – even when abstracted from a story – are not in themselves narrative; rather they are 'designed to account for the initial articulations of meaning within a semantic micro-universe' (Greimas 1970, p. 161. Culler's translation 1975, p. 92).[6] This is also why I shall discuss deep structure more briefly than surface structure.

DEEP NARRATIVE STRUCTURE

To my mind, the most important models of deep structure are those developed by Lévi-Strauss (1968. Orig. publ. in French 1958) and Greimas (1966, 1970, 1976). Although different in formalization, both consist of a correlation of two binary categories. True, Lévi-Strauss has not used the term 'deep structure', but Greimas, recognizing the affinity between the two models, rightly says:

> The distinction made by Lévi-Strauss, since his first study dedicated to myth, between an apparent signification of the myth, revealed in the textual narrative, and its deep meaning, paradigmatic and achronic, implies the same assumptions. . . . We therefore decided to give to the structure evolved by Lévi-Strauss the status of deep narrative structure, capable, in the process of syntagmatization, of generating a surface structure corresponding roughly to the syntagmatic chain of Propp.
>
> (1971, p. 796)[7]

According to Lévi-Strauss, the structure which underlies every myth is that of a four-term homology, correlating one pair of opposed mythemes with another.[8] The emerging formula is: A : B :: C : D : (A is to what B what C is to D). In the Oedipus myth, for example, the first opposition is between the overrating of blood relations (e.g. Oedipus marries his mother, Antigone buries her brother in spite of the interdiction) and its underrating (e.g. Oedipus kills his father, Oteocles kills his brother). The second opposition is between a negation of man's autochthonous origin (i.e. his being self-born, or sprung from the earth), and its affirmation. The negation is implied by various victories over autochthonous creatures, like the dragon and the sphinx, while the affirmation is suggested by several human defects (autochthony implying imperfection): Oedipus' swollen foot, Laius' name connoting left-sidedness, etc. The correlation of the two pairs of opposites 'says' that 'the overrating of blood relations is to the underrating of blood relations as the attempt to escape autochthony is to the impossibility to succeed in it' (1968, p. 216). The myth makes the problem of autochthony easier to grapple with by relating it to another, more common contradiction (for a more detailed discussion see Scholes 1974, pp. 68–74; Culler 1975, pp. 40–54; Hawkes 1977, pp. 39–43).

Whereas the two pairs of opposites in Lévi-Strauss's homology are of the same kind, Greimas puts into play two kinds of opposed semes (the 'seme' being the minimal unit of sense): contradictories and contraries. Contradictories (A v. not-A) are created when one seme (or – in logic – one proposition) negates the other, so that they cannot both be true and they cannot both be false. They are mutually exclusive and exhaustive (e.g. 'white' v. 'non-white'). Contraries, on the other hand (A v. B), are mutually exclusive but not exhaustive (e.g. 'white' v. 'black'). They cannot both be true, though they might both be false (Copi 1961, pp. 142–3). Replacing 'A' and 'B' by 'S1' and 'S2' (the 'S' standing for 'seme'), Greimas presents the 'semiotic square' thus:

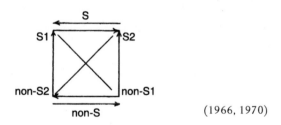

(1966, 1970)

In the universe of the French novelist Bernanos, for example, S1 and S2 are 'life' and 'death', and the square takes the following form:

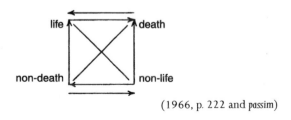

(1966, p. 222 and *passim*)

The same values can be manifested differently in different texts. Thus Greimas juxtaposes the 'life'/'death' opposition in Bernanos to the same opposition in Maupassant:

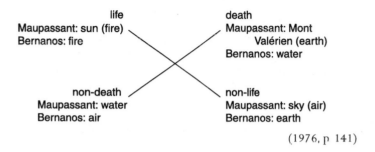

life
Maupassant: sun (fire)
Bernanos: fire

death
Maupassant: Mont
    Valérien (earth)
Bernanos: water

non-death
Maupassant: water
Bernanos: air

non-life
Maupassant: sky (air)
Bernanos: earth

(1976, p 141)

SURFACE NARRATIVE STRUCTURE

The problem of description

As stated earlier, story (including its surface structure) is a construct and an abstraction from the set of observable signifiers which is the text, and is thus intangible in itself. This creates a methodological difficulty for the poetics of narrative: how can the intangible be presented? Tangibility, or at least explicitness, it seems, can be given to the abstracted construct by writing it down as a paraphrase, and it is therefore with paraphrases that story-analysts work.

But what does a story-paraphrase consist of? One approach, stressing the similarity of paraphrase to the spontaneous activity of the reader, sees the former as a series of *event labels*. In S/Z Barthes treats the activity of event-labelling as one of the five codes of reading (on the codes see Culler 1975, pp. 202–3; Hawkes 1977, pp. 116–18, and chapter 9 below), calling it 'proairetic':

> . . . the proairetic sequence is never more than the result of an artifice of reading; whoever reads the text amasses certain data under some generic titles for actions (*stroll, murder, rendez-vous*), and this title embodies the sequence; the sequence exists when and because it can

be given a name, it unfolds as this process of naming takes place, as a title is sought or confirmed.

(1974, p. 19. Orig. publ. in French 1970.
See also Culler 1975, p. 220)

The labels given to events in reading or in a story-paraphrase are not necessarily identical with the language used in the text. This poses the problem of non-uniform labelling. If an event is described in the text as 'A blast was heard' or 'His fingers pressed the trigger', it can be labelled variously as Pressing a Trigger, Firing, Shot, Hit (or Miss), Killing, Success (or Failure), Homicide, Murder, Revenge, Crime, Misdeed, Violation, Breakdown of Order (or Re-Establishment of Order). The difference in label may depend on the level of abstraction, the purpose of the paraphrase, and the integration of other items of information from the text. The reader may assign any of the above labels at different points in the reading process according to the needs of intelligibility. As he progresses, he may also change a label he gave an event at an earlier stage of his reading. But more is required of the critic or the narratologist: he must be able to abstract homogeneous paraphrases, providing a consistent representation of the logical and semantic relations among all the events included. Some attempts along these lines have been made (see pp. 20–5), but the problem of uniformity keeps cropping up.

So far I have adopted one approach to story-paraphrases, discussing events in terms of labels. But it is evident that these leave out some information necessary for the intelligibility of what happens in the story. An apparently coherent sequence of actions identified by the event-labels Shooting, Wounding, Killing, would lose much of its coherence if the participants did not remain constant (if the shooter were not the killer or the wounded person not the one who was killed). Since any event involves one or more participants, the second approach suggests that instead of merely naming an event (giving it a label) it would be better to paraphrase it as a simple sentence. Like the labels discussed above, these simple sentences, called narrative propositions, are different from the sentences of the text (Todorov 1977, p. 112; Greimas 1977, p. 29. Orig. publ. in French 1969).[9]

Whether consisting of labels or of narrative propositions, a story-paraphrase arranges events according to a chronological principle. If the content-paraphrase abstracted from a text is organized according to principles other than chronological then it is not a story-paraphrase and the text in question is not a narrative. Descriptive or expository propositions, for example, are distinct from narrative ones in that they are thought of as simultaneously valid according to some *spatial* or *logical* principle which is relatively or ideally independent of temporality (Tomashevsky 1965, p. 66. Orig. publ. in Russian 1925). This is the case of the fine specimen of a non-narrative text already quoted in the introduction: 'Roses are red/Violets are blue/Sugar is sweet/And so are you'. All four propositions are simultaneously true; there is no temporal succession in the 'world' represented by these statements, and hence no story (Prince 1980, p. 49).

The presence or absence of a story is what distinguishes narrative from non-narrative texts. However, non-story elements may be found in a narrative text just as story elements may be found in a non-narrative text. A novel may well include the description of a cathedral, and the description of a cathedral, say in a guide book, may include the story of its construction.

The constitutive units of the surface structure

The description of the paraphrase as consisting of event-labels or of propositions constructed around events implies that the events themselves are the constituent units of the story.[10]

An event is defined by the OED as a 'thing that happens', and it is with such a vague notion that I began in the introduction. To make this a bit more useful for the purpose of the present study, one might add that when something happens, the situation usually changes. An event, then, may be said to be a change from one state of affairs to another. Unlike Chatman (1978, pp. 31–2), 1 do not insist on an opposition between state and event (or stasis and process), because it seems to me that an account of an event may be broken down into an infinite number of intermediary states. This is why a narrative text or a story-paraphrase need not include any sentence denoting a dynamic event; a succession of states would imply a succession of events, as it does in 'He was rich, then he was poor, then he was rich again.'[11] Just as any single event may be decomposed into a series of mini-events and intermediary states, so-conversely – a vast number of events may be subsumed under a single event-label (e.g. 'The Fall of the Roman Empire'). This is why it may be difficult at times to maintain an absolute distinction between the notion of 'event' and that of 'succession of events'.

Events can be classified into two main kinds: those that advance the action by opening an alternative ('kernels') and those that expand, amplify, maintain or delay the former ('catalysts') (Barthes 1966, pp. 9–10; Chatman 1969, pp. 3, 14–19. Chatman 1978 calls the second type 'satellites'). If a telephone rings, a character can either answer it or not; an alternative is opened and the event is therefore a kernel. But between the ringing of the phone and the answer (or the decision not to answer), the character may scratch his head, light a cigarette, curse, etc. These are catalysts – they do not open an alternative but 'accompany' the kernel in various ways.

Structural descriptions show how *events* combine to create *micro-sequences* which in turn combine to form *macro-sequences* which jointly create the complete story. Between the macro-sequences and the story, it is sometimes convenient to disengage an intermediary unit which may be called '*story-line*'. A story-line is structured like the complete story, but unlike the latter it is restricted to one set of individuals. Thus in *King Lear* one can distinguish the story-line involving Lear and his daughters from the one concerning Gloucester and his sons, although the two often intersect. Once a succession of events involving the same individuals establishes itself as the predominant story element of a text (and, unfortunately, there are no clear-cut criteria for predominance), it becomes the *main story-line*. A succession of events which involves another set of individuals is a *subsidiary story-line*.

Principles of combination

How are events combined into sequences and sequences into a story? The two main principles of combination are temporal succession and causality.

Time

As Todorov points out (1966, p. 127), the notion of story-time involves a convention which identifies it with ideal chronological order, or what is sometimes called 'natural chronology'. In fact, strict succession can only be found in stories with a single line or even with a single character. The minute there is more than one character, events may become simultaneous and the story is often multilinear rather than unilinear. Strict linear chronology, then, is neither natural nor an actual characteristic of most stories. It is a conventional 'norm' which has become so widespread as to replace the actual multilinear temporality of the story and acquire a pseudo-natural status.

Causality

Temporal succession, the 'and then' principle, is often coupled with the principle of causality − 'that's why' or 'therefore'. Half a century ago Forster used these two combinatory principles to distinguish between two types of narrative which he called respectively 'story' and 'plot':

> We have defined story as a narrative of events arranged in time-sequence. A plot is also a narrative of events, the emphasis falling on causality. 'The king died and then the queen died' is a story. 'The king died and then the queen died of grief' is a plot.
>
> (1963, p. 93. Orig. publ. 1927)[12]

But there is nothing to prevent a causally-minded reader from supplementing Forster's first example with the causal link that would make it into an implicit plot (see also Chatman 1978, p. 46). Indeed, as Barthes points out, stories may be based on an implicit application of the logical error: *post hoc, ergo propter hoc* (1966, p. 10). By way of example we may cite the witty account of Milton's life where the humour resides precisely in the cause and effect relation which can be read into the explicit temporal succession. Milton wrote *Paradise Lost*, then his wife died, and then he wrote *Paradise Regained*.

Causality can either be implied by chronology or gain an explicit status in its own right. But the very notion of causality is by no means unproblematic. Without embarking on a philosophical discussion of the issue, it is worth noting that two quite different senses of the term are often used as if they were one. Suppose we want to know 'why' in the early part of Dickens's *Great Expectations* (1860/61) the six- or seven-year-old Pip aids the runaway convict. Two different kinds of answer are possible: (1) according to the logic of verisimilitude (made prominent, in fact, by the text): the child was frightened into submission; (2) according to the structural needs of the plot: this act is necessary for Magwitch to be grateful to Pip so as to wish to repay him; without it the plot would not be the kind of plot it is. The second type is in fact teleological (i.e. concerned with purpose), but teleology of this kind is often grasped as 'forward causality', i.e. as distinct from the 'backward causality' of the first type.

Time, causality and the notion of minimal story

Are the two combinatory principles equally necessary to turn a group of events into a story, or is one more basic than the other? Here is Prince's definition of a minimal story:

> A minimal story consists of three conjoined events. The first and the third events are stative, the second is active. Furthermore, the third event is the inverse of the first. Finally, the three events are conjoined by conjunctive features in such a way that (a) the first event precedes the second in time and the second precedes the third, and (b) the second causes the third.
>
> (1973, p. 31)

An example of a minimal story provided by Prince is: 'He was rich, then he lost lots of money, then, as a result, he was poor.'[13] The above definition requires three principles of organization: (1) temporal succession; (2) causality; (3) inversion (which I take to be one of several forms of closure based on symmetry or balance).

While granting that causality and closure (i.e. a sense of completion) may be the most interesting features of stories, and the features on which their quality as stories is most often judged, I would like to argue that temporal succession is sufficient as a *minimal* requirement for a group of events to form a story. My argument is based on: (1) the above suggestion that causality can often (always?) be projected onto temporality; and (2) the counter-intuitive nature of Prince's requirements. If, like him, we posit causality and closure (through inversion, repetition, or analogy) as obligatory criteria, many groups of events which we intuitively recognize as stories would have to be excluded from this category.

Take, for instance, Chekhov's 'Lady with Lapdog' (1927. Orig. publ. in Russian 1899) which may be summarily paraphrased as follows: 'Gurov meets Anna Sergeyevna in Yalta, then they have an affair, then he returns to his family in Moscow, she to her husband in a provincial town, then Gurov goes to her town to seek her out, then they resume their affair in Moscow.' This, I believe, would be recognized by readers as a story, although it lacks Prince's conjunctive feature 'as a result'. One could, of course, supply causal connections by writing into the paraphrase propositions like 'he is unhappy', followed by a causal conjunction like '*therefore* he seeks her out', or 'she is still in love with him, *therefore* she comes to Moscow.' However, not only can the story be recognized as story even without them, but the text goes a long way toward preventing such causal connections from becoming obvious and presenting the conjunction of events as inevitable but not necessarily causal. Likewise, the chain of events does not display any obvious inversion or closed cycle: the state of affairs at the end is different from the initial one, but they are not symmetrically related (the characters are not 'happy' as opposed to 'unhappy' or vice versa). [14]

Does this mean that any two events, arranged in chronological order would constitute a story? Theoretically speaking, the answer must be Yes. True, temporal succession in itself is a rather loose link. Nevertheless, it implies that the events in question occur in the same represented world. There would indeed be something very odd about the following bit of story: 'Little Red Riding-Hood strays into the forest and then Pip aids the runaway convict.' But if we accept this as the possible paraphrase of *some* text (perhaps a narrative pastiche by Robert Coover or Donald Barthelme), then the temporal conjunction requires us to imagine some world where these events can co-exist. The link will become a bit tighter, without as yet becoming causal, if the same individuals (or a closely related group of individuals) remain constant as the participants in the series. For example: 'Don Quixote fights the windmills, then Don Quixote battles the gallant Basque, then Don Quixote converses with Sancho, then Don Quixote meets with the goatherds' etc.

Two descriptive models

Vladimir Propp

The aim of Propp's pioneering study (orig. publ. in Russian 1928) is to unearth the common pattern governing the narrative propositions abstracted from a corpus of close to two hundred Russian fairy tales (one type of folktale). For this purpose, the constant elements have to be abstracted from the variable, specific events and participants constituting the individual stories (as well as the propositions abstracted from them). The constant element is called a 'function', and its meaning for Propp is 'an act of a character, defined from the point of view of its significance for the course of the action' (1968, p. 21). Functions may remain constant even when the identity of the performer changes. Compare, for example, the following events:

1 A tsar gives an eagle to a hero. The eagle carries the hero away to another kingdom.
2 An old man gives Súcenko a horse. The horse carries Súcenko away to another kingdom.
3 A sorcerer gives Iván a little boat. The boat takes Iván to another kingdom.
4 A princess gives Iván a ring. Young men appearing from out of the ring carry Iván away into another kingdom, and so forth.

(Propp 1968, pp. 18–20)

The only constant element in all four cases is the transfer of someone by means of something obtained from someone to another kingdom. The identity of the participants in this event may change from tale to tale; both their names and their attributes are variable. This is why Propp insists that the study of *what* is done should precede 'the questions of who does it and how it is done' (p. 28).

But *what* is done may also contain a variable aspect: the same event, located at different points of the story, may fulfil different functions:

> if, in one instance, a hero receives money from his father in the form of 100 rubles and subsequently buys a wise cat with the money, whereas in the second case, the hero is rewarded with a sum of money for an accomplished act of bravery (at which point the tale ends), we have before us two morphologically different elements – in spite of the identical action (the transference of the money) in both cases.

(p. 21)

Consequently Propp labels his functions in a way that would express the differences in their contribution to the plot even when they are given the same designation in particular texts or when their general semantic content seems identical. Thus the first of the two events mentioned in the example is defined as 'Receipt of a Magical Agent' and occurs near the middle of the tale, whereas the second is a variant of a function labelled 'Marriage' (i.e. the hero's reward) which ends the tale.

The above explanation suggests (although Propp does not say this explicitly) that the choice of 'function' may have been motivated by two different dictionary senses of this term. In one sense, a function is the 'activity proper to anything, mode of action by which it fulfils its purpose', in this case its contribution to the plot. In another – logico-mathematical – sense, the term denotes a 'variable quantity in relation to others by which it may be expressed' (*OED*). This is appropriate because what Propp investigates are *propositional functions*, i.e. the common pattern of many singular propositions derived from the text of many particular stories.

Propp summarizes his conclusion in four points (the first of which I have already discussed):

1 Functions of the characters serve as stable, constant elements in a tale, regardless of how and by whom they are fulfilled.
2 The number of functions known to the fairy tale is limited.
3 The sequence of functions is always identical.
4 All fairy tales are of one type in regard to their structure.

(1968, pp. 21–3)

The number of functions, according to Propp, is thirty-one (see list 1968, pp. 26–63). They need not and in fact do not all occur in any one fairy tale. But those that do occur, always appear in the same order. This 'determinism' may be dictated by the material Propp analysed, but it may also be a bias caused by his method. Having defined a function by its contribution to the next function and having 'justified' this by the dictum 'Theft cannot take place before the door is forced' (p. 20), Propp is bound to find a constant order governing his functions. It is this, among other things, that Claude Bremond criticizes in Propp's theory.

Claude Bremond

Wishing to account for the possible bifurcations at each point of the story (even those that are not realized in the unfolding of a given tale), Bremond constructs a model which is more logically than temporally oriented (1966, 1973). After explicating the model, I shall present Ron's application of it to Sophocles' *Oedipus Rex*, a plot often praised for its tight logical structure. However, for the sake of clarity and illustration, I shall also draw on this application during the explication itself. Roughly speaking, the horizontal axis of the chart (see pp. 24–6) represents relations among states and events which are only logical, whereas the vertical axis represents relations that are both logical, and chronological.

As with Propp, the function is the basic unit for Bremond. Every three functions combine to form a sequence in which they punctuate three logical stages: possibility (or potentiality), process, and outcome.[15] Rather than automatically leading to the next function, as in Propp, each function opens two alternatives, two directions the story can subsequently take. This structure can be schematized in the form of a sort of horizontal tree:

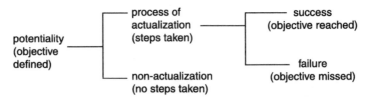

(Bremond 1966, p. 75. English translation modified)

The notion of bifurcation preserves a measure of freedom and allows for the description of plots where the Struggle with the Villain, for example, does not always end in Victory.[16] It may thus provide a formal ground for comparing different but related plot-patterns (e.g. comic v. tragic plots, folk-tale or romance v. ironic novellistic plots).

Such elementary sequences tend to combine into complex sequences in one of three ways:

1 Enchainment, or 'back to back' succession: the outcome (function 3) of one sequence amounts to (=) the potential stage (function 1) of the next. An example of this appears in Chart III: Oedipus' granting of the appeal is tantamount to a duty (or a promise) on his part, which opens a new sequence.

2 Embedding (Bremond's term is 'enclave'): one sequence is inserted into another as a specification or detailing of one of its functions. Bremond offers the following example:

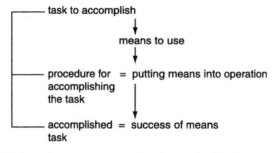

In Chart I below there is an example of an embedded sequence which is dominated by the second function (rather than by the first as in Bremond's example): Laius' attempt to ward off the dangers emanating from his son takes the form of (a) an intent to kill Oedipus, (b) an action taken to do so and (c) the failure of this action.

3 Joining: the same triad of events has a double narrative relevance and must be redundantly ranged under two character names. This relation is expressed by the symbol 'v.' (although Bremond sometimes, inconsistently, uses '='). Laius' sequence, used as example for type 2, is joined to Oedipus' survival sequence in this way, with each stage matched against its counterpart (really another label for the same state or event) in the other sequence. In this manner, what is an

The plot of Sophocles' Oedipus Rex according to Bremond's method (slightly modified)

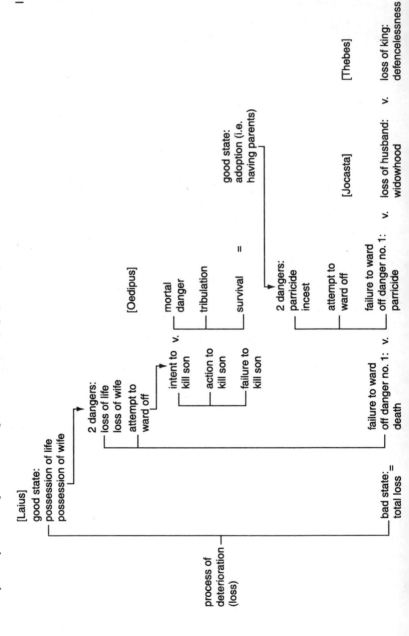

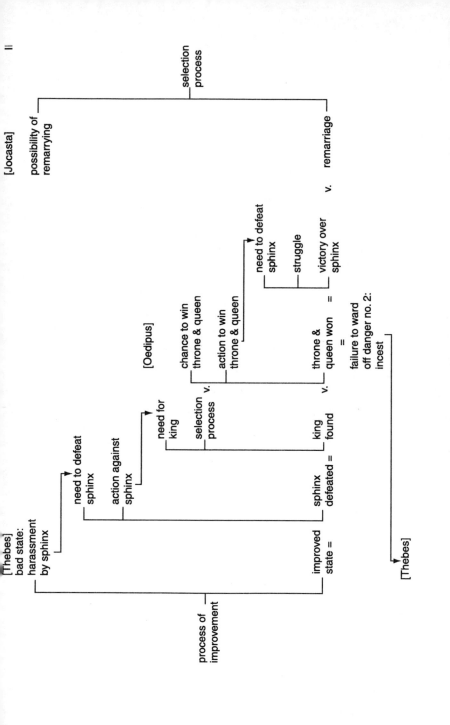

≡

[Thebes]
bad state:
plague

need for help
appeal for help
appeal granted

process of improvement

improved state

v.

[Oedipus]
bad state

duty to hear
hearing
appeal granted =

process of deterioration

tragic state

=

v.

duty to help
action to help

need for oracle
action to obtain oracle
oracle obtained =

need to punish murderer
punitive action

help extended

=

need to discover murderer
discovery procedure

murderer discovered

murderer punished

need to obtain evidence
process of obtaining evidence
evidence obtained

improvement in the state of one character may be *ipso facto* a deterioration in the state of another. Note that events affecting more than two characters seem to require additional axes. In the charts the number of axes is kept down by disregarding the perspectives of minor, although functional, characters like the shepherd and the messenger, and by inserting a third and fourth perspective horizontally as a *pis-aller*.

According to Bremond, all sequences, at least all macro-sequences, are either of improvement or of deterioration. An improvement sequence begins with a lack or a disequilibrium (e.g. a lack of a wife) and finally establishes equilibrium (e.g. finding a wife; marriage). This can be the end of the story, but when it is not, the equilibrium is disturbed (e.g. the wife runs away), and a process of deterioration follows. Reaching its rock bottom stage (e.g. divorce), this can give rise to further improvement (finding a new wife), and soon *ad infinitum* (at least in theory). Thus the first chart begins with a good state (Laius possesses both life and wife) and ends with a bad one (Laius dies). The second chart does the reverse (i.e. it begins with Thebes being harassed by the sphinx and ends with the defeat of the sphinx), and the third again begins with bad (plague) and ends with good (the city is saved). However, it should be noted that in ambiguous plots it may be impossible to classify states neatly into 'good' and 'bad'.

Having presented a few deep-structure and a few surface-structure models, the time has come to say that a complete model should also include the transformations leading from the former to the latter. Some work along these lines has been done (e.g. by Doležel 1971 and Greimas 1976), but further development is clearly called for. Even less work has been done on the transition from narrative structures to linguistic structures (if indeed there is such a transition).

Notes: Chart III represents action taking place on stage, I and II past events revealed during the stage action. Chart I and some aspects of II could possibly be embedded in III under 'process of obtaining evidence'. (2) For clarity's sake these charts disregard certain character perspectives and the sequences that go with them (Creon, Shepherd, Messenger). (3) This method cannot represent characters' awareness of the significance of events or any modalities of knowledge. Consequently Chart III ignores Thiresias and his prophecy. (4) This method does not strictly represent relations of succession and simultaneity between events.

Thus Greimas:

> It is the passage from level three where narrative objects are located to level two upon which linguistic discourses organized by narrativity are unravelled that the greatest difficulties in interpretation arise.
>
> (1971, p. 797)

I am not at all convinced that, from the reader's perspective, the passage from surface linguistic structures (1) to surface narrative structures (3) necessarily leads through deep linguistic structures (2). Several years ago a review of the state of the art concluded:

> Despite the variety of models, there is as yet no clear method of traversing the path from the concrete text to the abstract narrative structure, without either quantitative or qualitative gaps intervening.
>
> (Lipski 1976, p. 202)

To my knowledge, the situation has not changed significantly to date.

3

STORY: CHARACTERS

Whereas the study of the story's events and the links among them has been developed considerably in contemporary poetics, that of character has not. Indeed, the elaboration of a systematic, non-reductive but also non-impressionistic theory of character remains one of the challenges poetics has not yet met. My own contribution, however, falls short of this goal, and in the present chapter I shall indicate why this is so.

THE DEATH OF CHARACTER?

In addition to pronouncements about the death of God, the death of humanism, the death of tragedy, our century has also heard declarations concerning the death of character. 'What is obsolescent in today's novel', says Barthes, 'is not the novelistic, it is the character; what can no longer be written is the Proper Name' (1974, p. 95. Orig. publ. in French 1970).

Various features which had been considered the hallmarks of character, modelled on a traditional view of man, were denied to both by many modern novelists. Thus Alain Robbe-Grillet (1963, pp. 31–3) rejected 'the archaic myth of depth' and with it the psychological conception of character. Objecting not only to the notion of psychological depth but also to the corollary one of individuality, Nathalie Sarraute focused on an 'anonymous', 'pre-human' stratum underlying all individual variations. Her reader, she hoped, would be 'plunged and remain immersed to the end in a substance as anonymous as blood, in a magma without name, without contour' (1965, p. 74. Orig. publ. 1956. My translation). (And quite a bit earlier, in his 1914 letter to Edward Garnett, D. H. Lawrence protested against, the old-fashioned human element' and declared:

> I don't so much care about what the woman *feels* – in the ordinary usage of the word. That presumes an ego to feel with. I only care about what the woman *is* – what she IS – inhumanly, physiologically, materially. . . .
>
> (in Aldous Huxley (ed.) 1932, p. 198)

Together with the rejection of individuality in favour of 'carbon', the underlying non-human, quasi-chemical element, Lawrence also substituted for the notion of the persistence of traits that of 'allotropic states', thus calling into question the belief in the ego's stability.[1] Additional conceptions of change and diversity replaced the notion of stability in the writing of other modern novelists. Virginia Woolf for example, saw character (and life in general) as a flux and wanted to 'record the atoms as they fall upon the mind' (1953, pp. 153–5. Orig. publ. 1925). And Hélène Cixous questions not only the stability but also the unity of the self. The 'I', according to her, is 'always more than one, diverse, capable of being all those it will at one time be, a group acting together' (1974, p.387). If the self is a constant flux or if it is a 'group acting together', the concept of character changes or disappears, the 'old stable ego' disintegrates.

Character, then, is pronounced 'dead' by many modern writers. Nails are added to its coffin by various contemporary theorists. Structuralists can hardly accommodate character within their theories, because of their commitment to an ideology which 'decentres' man and runs counter to the notions of individuality and psychological depth:[2]

> Stress on the interpersonal and conventional systems which traverse the individual, which make him a space in which forces and events

meet rather than an individuated essence, leads to a rejection of a prevalent conception of character in the novel: that the most successful and 'living' characters are richly delineated autonomous wholes, clearly distinguished from others by physical and psychological characteristics. The notion of character, structuralists would say, is a myth.

(Culler 1975, p. 230)

But is character as 'dead' as all that? Do the new views dispense with it altogether, or do they only dismantle a certain traditional concept of it? Can the changing notions be seen as nevertheless leaving some constitutive characteristics recognizable? Isn't Joyce's Bloom a character in some sense of the word? And do not even the minimal depersonalized characters of some modern fiction 'deserve' a non-reductive theory which will adequately account for their place and functioning within the narrative network? Moreover, even if we grant the 'death' of character in contemporary literature, can we also retrospectively 'kill' him in nineteenth-century fiction? Should a non-humanist, anti-bourgeois ideology (even if it is accepted) lead us to ignore that which is plainly central in a given corpus of narratives? The development of a theory of character, I believe, has been impeded not only by the ideology of this or that 'school' of poetics, or this or that 'fashion' in literature, but by more basic problems to which I now turn.

THE MODE OF EXISTENCE OF CHARACTER: TWO PROBLEMS

People or words?

Already in 1961 Marvin Mudrick had formulated the two extreme views of character suggested in the title of this section, and discerned a shift from one to the other which has become much more conspicuous since he wrote:

One of the recurring anxieties of literary critics concerns the way in which a character in drama or fiction may be said to exist. The 'purist' argument – in the ascendancy nowadays among critics – points out that characters do not exist at all except insofar as they are a part of the images and events which bear and move them, that any effort to extract them from their context and to discuss them as if they are real human beings is a sentimental misunderstanding of the nature of literature. The 'realistic' argument – on the defensive nowadays – insists that characters acquire, in the course of an action, a kind of independence from the events in which they live, and that they can be usefully discussed at some distance from their context.

(p. 211)

As emerges from Mudrick's statement, the so-called 'realistic' argument sees characters as imitations of people and tends to treat them – with greater or lesser sophistication – as if they were our neighbours or friends, whilst also abstracting them from the verbal texture of the work under consideration. Such an approach, of which Bradley's analyses of Shakespeare's characters (1965. Orig. publ. 1904) is perhaps the best known example, tends to speculate about the characters' unconscious motivations and even constructs for them a past and future beyond what is specified in the text.[3] A position of this kind facilitates the construction of a theory of character because it legitimizes the transference of ready-made theories from psychology or psychoanalysis. However, it is precisely for this reason that such an analysis fails to discover the *differentia specifica* of characters in narrative fiction.

That the *differentia specifica* are of a verbal and non-representational order is what the so-called 'purist' (nowadays we would probably say 'semiotic') argument emphasizes. An extreme formulation of this argument, however, assimilates character to other verbal phenomena in the text to the extent of destroying its specificity in its own way:

Under the aegis of semiotic criticism, characters lose their privilege, their central status, and their definition. This does not mean that they are metamorphosed into inanimate things (à la Robbe-Grillet) or reduced to actants (à la Todorov) but that they are textualized. As segments of a closed text, characters at most are patterns of recurrence, motifs which are continually recontextualized in other motifs. In semiotic criticism, characters dissolve.

(Weinsheimer 1979, p. 195)

To demonstrate his point, Weinsheimer analyses the ways in which Jane Austen's Emma, traditionally considered one of the most 'person-like' characters in English literature, is textualized. In the course of the analysis, he makes the following provocative statement: 'Emma Woodhouse is not a woman nor need be described as if it were' (1979, p. 187. The 'it', of course, is telling).

Whereas in mimetic theories (i.e. theories which consider literature as, in some sense, an imitation of reality) characters are equated with people, in semiotic theories they dissolve into textuality. What remains? If both approaches end up cancelling the specificity of fictional characters, though from different standpoints, should the study of character be abandoned, or should both approaches be rejected and a different perspective sought? Can such a perspective reconcile the two opposed positions without 'destroying' character between them? Is it possible to see characters 'at once as persons and as parts of a design' (Price 1968, p. 290)? I think it is, provided one realizes that the two extreme positions can be thought of as relating to different aspects of narrative fiction. In the text characters are nodes in the verbal design; in the story they are – by definition – non (or pre-) verbal abstractions, constructs. Although these constructs are by no means human beings in the literal sense of the word, they are partly modelled on the reader's conception of people and in this they are person-like.

Similarly, in the text, characters are inextricable from the rest of the design, whereas in the story they are extracted from their textuality. This not only follows from the definition of story but is also borne out by experience:

> The equation of characters with 'mere words' is wrong on other grounds. Too many mimes, too many captionless silent films, too many ballets have shown the folly of such a restriction. Too often do we recall fictional characters vividly, yet not a single word of the text in which they came alive; indeed, I venture to say that readers generally remember characters that way.
>
> (Chatman 1978, p. 118)

Moreover, as abstractions from the text, character names often serve as 'labels' for a trait or cluster of traits characteristic of non-fictional human beings, e.g. 'he is a Hamlet'. Even Weinsheimer, whose extreme, one-sided view was quoted above, ends his article with a recognition of the complex status of character. He now talks about 'the textualized persons, personified texts that are characters' (p. 208).

Being or doing

Another problem is the subordination of character to action or its relative independence of it. Aristotle, it is known, believed characters to be necessary only as 'agents' or 'performers' of the action (1951, p. 34), a view shared by formalists and structuralists of our own century, though for different reasons. In addition to the decentring of man discussed above, methodological considerations also lead to such subordination. Like any scientifically oriented discipline, formalist and structuralist poetics recognizes the methodological necessity of reduction, especially in preliminary phases of an inquiry. Since action seems more easily amenable to the construction of 'narrative grammars' (often based on verb-centred grammars of natural languages), it is convenient to reduce character to action – at least in the first stage.

Thus Propp (1968. Orig. publ. in Russian 1928) subordinates characters to 'spheres of action' within which their performance can be categorized according to seven general roles: the villain, the donor, the helper, the sought-for-person and her father, the dispatcher, the hero and the false hero. In a given narrative, a character may perform more than one role (e.g. Magwitch in *Great Expectations* first appears as villain, later as donor and helper) and conversely, a role may be fulfilled by more than one character (e.g. there is more than one villain in *Great Expectations*).

In a similar vein, Greimas (1966, 1973, 1979) indicates the subordination of characters by calling them '*actants*'. In fact, he distinguishes between '*acteur*' and '*actant*', but both are conceived of as accomplishing or submitting to an act (1979, p. 3) and both can include not only human beings (i.e. 'characters') but also inanimate objects (e.g. a magic ring) and abstract concepts (e.g. destiny). The difference between the two is that *actants* are general categories underlying all narratives (and not only narratives) while *acteurs* are invested with specific qualities in different narratives. Thus, *acteurs* are numerous, whereas the number of *actants* is reduced to six in Greimas's model:

$$\text{sender} \rightarrow \text{object} \rightarrow \text{receiver}$$
$$\uparrow$$
$$\text{helper} \rightarrow \text{subject} \leftarrow \text{opponent}$$

The same *actant* can be manifested by more than one *acteur*, and the same *acteur* can be assigned to more than one *actant*. To illustrate: in the sentence 'Pierre and Paul give an apple to Mary', Pierre and Paul – two *acteurs* – are one *actant*: sender, Mary is another: receiver. The apple is the object (Hamon 1977, p. 137. Orig. publ. 1972).[4] On the other hand, in the sentence 'Pierre buys himself a coat', one *acteur* (Pierre) functions as two *actants* (sender and receiver).

It is not only so-called traditional critics who tend to reverse the hierarchy between action and character discussed above; some structuralists also envisage this possibility. Thus whereas in 1966 Barthes clearly subordinates character to action (pp. 15–18), in 1970 he gives character a separate code (the semic code) and even ponders the possibility that 'what is proper to narrative is not action but the character as a Proper Name' (1974, p. 131).[5] And Ferrara attempts to construct a model for a structural analysis of narrative fiction with character as the central notion:

> In fiction the character is used as the structuring element: the objects and the events of fiction exist – in one way or another – because of the character and, in fact, it is only in relation to it that they possess those qualities of coherence and plausibility which make them meaningful and comprehensible.
>
> (1974, p. 252)

Can the opposed views be reconciled? Again I would answer in the positive, for several reasons. First, instead of subordinating character to action or the other way round, it may be possible to consider the two as interdependent. This indeed is the thrust of Henry James's famous dictum: 'What is character but the determination of incident? What is incident but the illustration of character?' (1963, p. 80. Orig. publ. 1884). The forms of this interdependence, however, remain to be analysed.

Second, the opposed subordinations can be taken as relative to types of narrative rather than as absolute hierarchies. There are narratives in which character predominates (so-called psychological narratives) and others in which action does (apsychological narratives) (Todorov 1977, p. 67. Orig. publ. in French 1971). Raskolnikov's actions serve mainly to characterize him, whereas Sinbad's 'character' exists only for the sake of the action. Between the two extremes, there are – of course – different degrees of predominance of one or the other element.

Third, the reversibility of hierarchies may be postulated as a general principle extending beyond the question of genres or types of narrative (Hrushovski 1974, pp. 21–2; 1976a, p. 6). Depending on the element on which the reader focuses his attention, he may at various points subsume the available information under different hierarchies. Thus characters may be subordinated to action when action is the centre of attention, but action can become subordinate to character as soon as the reader's interest shifts to the latter. Different hierarchies may be established in different readings of the same text but also at different points within the same reading. The reversibility of hierarchies is characteristic not only of ordinary reading but also of literary criticism and theory. Hence it is legitimate to subordinate character to action when we study action but equally legitimate to subordinate action to character when the latter is the focus of our study.

HOW IS CHARACTER RECONSTRUCTED FROM THE TEXT?

I have said above that in the story character is a construct, put together by the reader from various indications dispersed throughout the text.[6] This 'putting together' or reconstruction is described by Barthes as part of the 'process of nomination' which, in his view, is synonymous with the act of reading:

> To read is to struggle to name, to subject the sentences of a text to a semantic transformation. This transformation is erratic; it consists in

hesitating among several names: if we are told that Sarrasine had *'one of those strong wills that know no obstacle'*, what are we to read? *will, energy, obstinacy, stubbornness*, etc.?

(1974, p. 92)

According to Chatman (1978), who develops Barthes's views in his own way, what is named in the case of character are personality traits.[7] Indeed, for Chatman character is a paradigm of traits, 'trait' being defined as a 'relatively stable or abiding personal quality' and 'paradigm' suggesting that the set of traits can be seen 'metaphorically, as a vertical assemblage intersecting the syntagmatic chain of events that comprise the plot' (1978, p. 127). Using a linguistic analogy, Chatman describes a trait as 'a narrative adjective tied to the narrative copula' (i.e. the equivalent of the verb 'to be') (1978, p. 125). Thus, 'Sarrasine is feminine', 'Othello is jealous', are examples of what Chatman calls 'trait'. It is probably this type of link between the character and the quality that leads Garvey (1978, p. 73) to speak of the reconstruction of character in terms of 'attributive propositions'. (An attributive proposition, according to him, consists of a character's name (or its equivalent), a predicate (e.g. 'insane') and a 'modalizer', indicating degrees and qualifications (e.g. 'questionable', 'to some extent') (1978, p. 73).

The transition from textual element to abstracted trait or attributive proposition is not always and not necessarily as immediate as would seem to emerge from the studies mentioned above. On the contrary, it is often mediated by various degrees of generalization. Following Hrushovski (forthcoming), I would like to suggest that the construct called character can be seen as a tree-like hierarchical structure in which elements are assembled in categories of increasing integrative power.[8] Thus an elementary pattern may be established by linking two or more details within a unifying category, e.g. a character's daily visits to his mother may be grouped together with his daily quarrels with her and generalized as 'X's relations with his mother', perhaps with the additional label 'ambivalence'. But elements can be subordinated to more than one pattern. X's quarrels with his mother, for example, can also be grouped together with his other quarrels (rather than with other manifestations of his relations with his mother) and generalized as, say, 'X's foul temper'.

For the moment, however, let us cling to the first pattern. The character's relations with his mother can subsequently be combined with similar generalizations about his relations with his wife, his boss, his friends, to form a higher category labelled 'X's relations with people'. This category in turn can be combined with other aspects of the same order of generalization, e.g. X's worldview, manner of speech, actions. These, of course, are not only aspects of character but also potential constituents of non-character constructs, such as the work's ideology, style, action. If a common denominator, e.g. ambivalence, emerges from several aspects, it can then be generalized as a character-trait, and in a similar way the various traits combine to form the character. A trait is sometimes explicitly mentioned in the text and sometimes not. When it is, the textual label may confirm the one reached in the process of generalization, but it may also be at variance with it, creating tension whose effects vary from one narrative to another. To give only one example: 'independence' is one of the labels constantly mentioned in connection with Isabel Archer in James's *The Portrait of a Lady* (1881). However, the reader gradually realizes that this independent lady's career is actually made up of a series of unwitting dependences. She depends on Mrs Touchett to get her to England, on Ralph's money to be able to establish the kind of life she thinks she wants, and on Mme Merle and Osmond to become the latter's wife. The clash between the textual label and the reader's conclusions adds to the poignancy and irony of Isabel's fate.

The reader need not always go through all these stages; he can skip a few with the help of a 'hunch'. Moreover, the hierarchy (like all hierarchies, according to Hrushovski) is reversible. Thus, a character's relations with his wife may be subordinated to the trait labelled 'jealousy', but on the other hand 'jealousy' may be subordinated to the character's relations with his wife (which include other features as well). In addition to reversibility within the character-construct, elements or patterns of this construct may entertain a relation of reversibility with other hierarchical constructs. Thus, just as various instances of X's ambivalence can be subordinated to this trait in his character, so the trait itself can be subsumed (together with the ambivalence of other characters or with situations of ambiguity) under a theme or a world view revolving around ambivalence.

When, in the process of reconstruction, the reader reaches a point where he can no longer integrate an element within a constructed category, the implication would seem to be either that the generalization established so far has been mistaken (a mistake which the text may have encouraged), or that the character has changed. Such a view allows for a discussion of the 'directional' dimension of character (development, 'biography'),whereas Chatman's 'paradigm of traits' makes character a more static construct.[9]

On what basis are elements combined in increasingly broader categories, culminating with the more or less unified construct called 'character'? A fundamental cohesive factor is the proper name. To quote Barthes again:

> Character is an adjective, an attribute, a predicate . . . Sarrasine is the sum, the point of convergence, of: *turbulence, artistic gift, independence, excess, femininity, ugliness, composite nature, impiety, love of whittling, will,* etc. What gives the illusion that the sum is supplemented by a precious remainder (something like *individuality,* in that, qualitative and ineffable, it may escape the vulgar bookkeeping of compositional characters) is the Proper Name, the difference completed by what is *proper* to it. The proper name enables the person to exist outside the semes, whose sum nonetheless constitutes it entirely. As soon as a Name exists (even a pronoun to flow toward and fasten onto), the semes become predicates, inductors of truth, and the Name becomes a subject.
>
> (1974, pp. 190–1)

How are elements combined into unifying categories under the aegis of the proper name? The main principles of cohesion, it seems to me, are repetition, similarity, contrast, and implication (in the logical sense). The repetition of the same behaviour 'invites' labelling it as a character-trait, as can be seen in Faulkner's 'A Rose for Emily' (1930) where the heroine's repeated Sunday rides with Homer Baron suggest both her defiance of the townspeople and her stubbornness. Similarities of behaviour on different occasions, like Emily's refusal to admit the death of her father and her preservation of her ex-lover's corpse, also give rise to a generalization, in this case her clinging to people who robbed her of her life (as the townspeople interpret it), or her necrophilia. Contrast is not less conducive to generalization than similarity, as when a character's ambivalence toward his mother emerges from the tension between his frequent visits to her and his equally frequent quarrels with her. As to implication, three of its forms are mentioned by Garvey (1978, pp. 74–5): (1) 'a set of physical attributes implies a psychological AP (Attributive Proposition)', e.g. X bites his fingernails → X is nervous; (2) 'a set of psychological attributions implies a further psychological AP', e.g. X hates his father and loves his mother → X has an Oedipus complex; (3) 'a set of psychological and physical attributes implies a psychological AP', e.g. X sees a snake, X becomes fearful → X is afraid of snakes.

The unity created by repetition, similarity, contrast, and implication may, of course, be a unity in diversity; it still contributes to the cohesion of various traits around the proper name, on which the effect we call 'character' depends.

CHARACTER-CLASSIFICATION

The various characters abstracted from a given text are seldom grasped as having the same degree of 'fullness'. Already in 1927 Forster recognized this, distinguishing between 'flat' and 'round' characters. Flat characters are analogous to 'humours', caricatures, types. 'In their purest form, they are constructed around a single idea or quality' and therefore 'can be expressed in one sentence' (1963, p. 75. Orig. publ. 1927). Furthermore, such characters do not develop in the course of the action. As a consequence of the restriction of qualities and the absence of development, flat characters are easily recognized and easily remembered by the reader. Round characters are defined by contrastive implication, namely those that are not flat. Not being flat involves having more than one quality and developing in the course of the action.

Forster's distinction is of pioneering importance, but it also suffers from a few weaknesses: (1) The term 'flat' suggests something two-dimensional, devoid of depth and 'life', while in fact many flat characters, like those of Dickens, are not only felt as very much 'alive' but also create the impression of depth. (2) The dichotomy is highly reductive, obliterating the degrees and nuances found in actual works of narrative fiction. (3) Forster seems to confuse two criteria which do not always overlap. According to him, a flat character is both simple and undeveloping, whereas a round character is both complex and developing. Although these criteria often co-exist, there are fictional characters which are complex but undeveloping (e.g. Joyce's Bloom) and others which are simple but developing (e.g. the allegorical Everyman). Moreover, the lack of development can be presented as arrested development resulting from some psychic trauma, as in the case of Miss Havisham in Dicken's *Great Expectations* (1860/61), thus endowing a static character with complexity.[10]

In order to avoid reductiveness, Ewen (1971, p. 7; 1980, pp. 33–44) suggests a classification of characters as points along a continuum rather than according to exhaustive categories.[11] And in order to keep the principle of classification clear, he advocates a distinction among three continua or axes: complexity, development, penetration into the 'inner life'. At one pole on the axis of *complexity* he locates characters constructed around a single trait or around one dominant trait along with a few secondary ones. Allegorical figures, caricatures, and types belong to this pole. In the first, the proper name represents the single trait around which the character is constructed (Pride, Sin). In the second, one out of the various qualities is exaggerated and made prominent (e.g. many of Gogol's characters). And in the third, the prominent trait is grasped as representative of a whole group rather than as a purely individual quality (e.g. Hirsch, the Jew, in Conrad's *Nostromo*, 1904). At the opposite pole Ewen locates complex characters like Dostoevsky's Raskolnikov or James's Isabel Archer. Between the two poles one can distinguish infinite degrees of complexity.

Allegorical figures, caricatures, and types are not only simple but also static, and can thus also occupy, together with 'portraits' of the Theophrastes or La Bruyère type, one pole on the axis of *development*. But static, undeveloping characters need not be limited to one trait; although static, Joe Gargery and Wemmick in *Great Expectations* clearly have more than one quality. Characters who do not develop are often minor, serving some function beyond themselves (e.g. representing the social milieu in which the major character acts). At the opposite pole there are fully developed characters, like Stephen in Joyce's *A Portrait of* the *Artist as a Young Man* (1916) or Strether in James's *The Ambassadors* (1903). The development is sometimes fully traced in the text, as in the two examples given above, and sometimes only implied by it, as when Miss Bates in Austen's *Emma* (1816) turns from a funny figure to a figure of pathos without a detailed tracing of the distance traversed.[12]

The third axis, *penetration into the 'inner life'* ranges from characters such as Woolf's Mrs Dalloway or Joyce's Molly Bloom, whose consciousness is presented from within, to the likes of Hemingway's killers (in the story bearing this name, 1928), seen only from the outside, their minds remaining opaque.[13]

Discussion of a character's 'inner life' is a far cry from referring to Emma Woodhouse as 'it' or treating characters as *'actants'* (see pp. 33–5). The co-presence of such contrasted concepts in this chapter is not an oversight or an inconsistency, but a gesture toward the reconciliation suggested earlier. Of course, co-presence is not in itself a reconciliation, and the very fact that it may be grasped as an inconsistency can serve as an indication of one aspect of the work that remains to be done before an integrated theory of character becomes feasible.

4

TEXT: TIME

Having insisted on the interdependence of the three aspects of narrative fiction in the introduction, and having analysed story in isolation in the two previous chapters, I shall now proceed to discuss text in its relation to story on the one hand and narration on the other. Three consecutive chapters will be devoted to three textual factors: time, characterization, focalization. The first two will be examined in relation to story: time as the textual arrangement of the event component of the story, and characterization as the representation in the text of the character component of the story. The third factor, focalization, is the angle of vision through which the story is filtered in the text, and it is verbally formulated by the narrator. This factor will therefore be studied mainly in relation to narration.

GENERAL CONSIDERATIONS

Time is one of the most basic categories of human experience. Doubts have been cast as to the validity of considering time a constituent of the physical world, but individuals and societies continue to experience time and to regulate their lives by it. Some of our notions of time are derived from natural processes: day and night, a solar year with its four seasons (but not in the arctic zone), etc. A person shut off from all perception of the outside world would still, presumably, continue to experience the *succession* of his own thoughts and feelings. In between these two extremes – the natural and the personal – is the mainstream of temporal experience: time as an intersubjective, public, social convention which we establish in order to facilitate our living together.

Our civilization tends to think of time as an uni-directional and irreversible flow, a sort of one-way street. Such a conception was given metaphoric shape by Heraclitus early in western history: 'You cannot step twice into the same river, for other waters and yet other waters go ever flowing on.' Today we might add that not only the object of experience but also the experiencing subject is in a constant flux. To become socialized, the flux must be made measurable. It can become measurable only when a repetitive pattern is discerned within it (e.g. the solar year) or imposed upon it by machines constructed too this end (calendar-, clock-, metronome-time). Time 'is', paradoxically, repetition within irreversible change. The repetitive aspect of time is sometimes taken one step further and seen as a refutation of Heraclitan unidirectionality, as in Nietzsche's and Borges's concepts of 'circular time'.

Like any other aspect of the world, the experience of time may be represented in a narrative text, as (for example) in Virginia Woolf's *To the Lighthouse* (1927). But time is not only a recurrent theme in a great deal of narrative fiction, it is also a constituent factor of both story and text. The peculiarity of verbal narrative is that in it time is constitutive both of the means of representation (language) and of the object represented (the incidents of the story).[1] Thus time in narrative fiction can be defined as the relations of chronology between story and text. To say this, however, is not only to define time but also to imply a few inescapable complications. We have already seen (pp. 16–17) that story-time, conceived of as a linear succession of events, is no more than a conventional, pragmatically convenient construct. Text-time is equally problematic. Strictly speaking, it is a spatial, not a temporal, dimension. The narrative text as text has no other temporality than the one it metonymically derives from the process of its reading. What discussions of text-time actually refer to is the linear (spatial) disposition of linguistic segments in the continuum of the text. Thus both story-time and text-time may in fact be no more than pseudo-temporal. Nevertheless, as long as we remember their 'pseudo' nature they remain useful constructs for the study of an important facet of the story-text relations.

The disposition of elements in the text, conventionally called text-time, is bound to be one-directional and irreversible, because language prescribes a linear figuration of signs and hence a linear presentation of information about things. We read letter after letter, word after word, sentence after sentence, chapter after chapter, and so on. There are some modern attempts to liberate narrative fiction from these constraints, but the liberation is never complete because a complete one, if possible, will destroy intelligibility. Thus in Beckett's *Watt* there are a few sections where Watt, at least partly demented, reverses the order of words in the sentence, letters in the word, sentences in the paragraph, etc. But the narrator explains these inversions to the reader before reproducing them, thus making it possible for him to recuperate the original order (1972, pp. 162–6. Orig. publ. in French 1953). Similarly, in *Hopscotch* (1967. Orig. publ. in Spanish 1963), the Argentine writer Julio Cortázar defies linearity by making the order of the *chapters* variable. In a 'Table of Instructions' preceding the novel, he writes:

> In its own way this book consists of many books, but two books above all.
> The first can be read in a normal fashion and ends with chapter 56. . . .
> The second should be read by beginning with chapter 73 and then following the sequence indicated at the end of each chapter. . . .

To illustrate this procedure, here is the beginning of the latter 'sequence': 73–1–2–116–3–84–4–71–5–81–74–6–7–8–93–68–9–104–10–65. But even here chapters 1–56 are to be read in order, with chapters 57–155 interspersed between them.

Text-time is thus inescapably linear, and therefore cannot correspond to the multilinearity of 'real' story-time.[2] But even when we compare text-time to the *conventional* story-time, i.e. to an ideal 'natural' chronology, we find that a hypothetical 'norm' of complete correspondence between the two is only rarely realized, and almost exclusively in very simple narratives. In practice, although the text always unfolds in linear succession, this need not correspond to the chronological succession of events, and most often deviates from it, creating various kinds of discordances. To my knowledge, the most exhaustive discussion of the discrepancies between story-time and text-time is Genette's (1972, pp. 77–182), and the following account will rely heavily on his, with some reservations, modifications and examples of my own.[3]

Time in general may be viewed in three respects: order, duration and frequency. Statements about *order* would answer the question 'when?' in terms like: first, second, last; before, after, etc. Statements about *duration* would answer the question 'how long?' in terms like: an hour, a year; long, short; from x till y, etc. Statements about *frequency* would answer the question 'how often?' in terms like: x times a minute, a month, a page. It is under these headings that Genette sets out to examine the relations between story-time and text-time.[4] Under *order* Genette discusses the relations between the succession of events in the story and their linear disposition in the text. Under *duration* he examines the relations between the time the events are supposed to have taken to occur and the amount of text devoted to their narration. Under *frequency* he looks at the relations between the number of times an event appears in the story and the number of times it is narrated in the text.

ORDER

The main types of discrepancy between story-order and text-order ('anachronies' in Genette's terms) are traditionally known as 'flash-back' or 'retrospection' on the one hand and 'foreshadowing' or 'anticipation' on the other. However, in order to avoid the psychological as well as the cinematic-visual connotations of these terms, I shall follow Genette in rebaptizing them 'analepsis' and 'prolepsis' respectively. An *analepsis* is a narration of a story-event at a point in the text after later events have been told. The narration returns, as it were, to a past point in the story. Conversely, a *prolepsis* is a narration of a story-event at a point before earlier events have been mentioned. The narration, as it were, takes an excursion into the future of the story. If events a, b, c figure in the text in the order b, c, a then 'a' is analeptic. If on the other hand, they appear in the order c, a, b then 'c' would be proleptic. Both analepsis and prolepsis constitute a temporally second narrative in relation to the narrative onto which they are grafted and which Genette calls 'first narrative'. The 'first narrative', then, is – somewhat circularly – 'the temporal level of narrative with respect to which an anachrony is defined as such' (1972, p. 90; 1980, p. 48).

Analepses provide past information either about the character, event, or story-line mentioned at that point in the text ('homodiegetic analepsis', according to Genette), or about another character, event, or story-line ('heterodiegetic analepsis') (the term *diegesis* is roughly analogous to my 'story'). The first type of analepsis can be illustrated by an example from Flaubert's *Sentimental Education*. Chapter 1, whose action takes place on 15 September 1840, ends with Frédéric's being summoned by a note from his friend Deslauriers to join him downstairs:

> Frédéric hesitated. But friendship won the day. He picked up his hat.
> 'Don't stay out too late, anyway', said his mother.
> (1970, p. 24. Orig. publ. in French 1869)

Chapter 2 begins as follows:

> Charles Deslauriers' father, a former infantry officer who had resigned his commission in 1818, had returned to Nogent to marry, and with his bride's dowry he had purchased a post as bailiff which was barely sufficient to keep him alive.
> (1970, p. 24)

The account of the father's past history is subordinate to that of Charles Deslauriers himself the main topic of the analysis: 'Few children were thrashed more frequently than his son, but beatings failed to break the lad's spirit' (p. 25), and so on.

Whereas the example from Flaubert is homodiegetic, i.e. referring mainly to Charles Deslauriers, Proust's *Un amour de Swann* (1919) is a heterodiegetic analepsis. Swann, who is only a minor character in the first section of *A la recherche du temps perdu*, a section whose action takes place during Marcel's boyhood, becomes the protagonist of the second section, whose action takes place long before Marcel's birth.

Both these analepses, though one is homodiegetic and one heterodi-egetic, evoke a past which precedes the starting point of the first narra-tive, hence they are 'external analepses' in Genette's terms. Other analepses may conjure up a past which 'occurred' after the starting point of the first narrative but is either repeated analeptically or narrated for the first time at a point in the text later than the place where it is 'due' ('internal analepses'). Such analepses often fill in a gap created previously, sometimes a gap which is not felt as such until it is filled-in in retrospect.[5] A well known example of internal analepsis is the account of Emma's years in the convent in Flaubert's *Madame Bovary* (1857). These years, summed up after later events in Emma's life have been told, are obviously posterior to Charles's first day at the new school, the starting point of the novel (Genette 1972, p. 98). If the period covered by the analepsis begins before the starting point of the first narrative but at a later stage either joins it or goes beyond it, then the analepsis is considered 'mixed'.

Prolepses are much less frequent than analepses, at least in the west-ern tradition. When they occur, they replace the kind of suspense deriv-ing from the question 'What will happen next?' by another kind of suspense, revolving around the question 'How is it going to happen?'[6] Prolepsis, in the strict sense of telling the future before its time, should be distinguished from a preparation of or a hinting at a future occur-rence ('*amorce*', in Genette's terms) of the type envisioned in Chekhov's famous dictum about the necessary connection between the presence of a gun on stage and a future murder or suicide. In a pure prolepsis the reader is confronted with the future event before its time, whereas a mere preparation of subsequent events is on the whole grasped as such only in retrospect. Experienced readers, of course, may easily recognize such information 'planted' for later use, especially in highly con-ventional genres. This phenomenon may call for the introduction of false preparations (Barthes's 'snares', 1974, p. 85. Orig. publ. in French 1970), e.g. a gun that is never used. These in turn may become a recognizable convention, calling for the introduction of false snares which are, in fact, true preparations, and so on.

On the whole, Genette argues, so-called first-person narratives[7] lend themselves to the use of prolepsis better than other types, because within the admittedly retrospective character of such narratives it seems more natural for the narrator to allude to a future which has already become a past. Thus the bulk of Borges's 'The Garden of Forking Paths' is said to be dictated by the spy-narrator a short time before his execution. From this vantage point, he narrates his own past as a spy and often anticipates what for his past self (and for the 'present' reader) was a future but is no longer so for his present narrating self. One example of this phenomenon will suffice:

> In the midst of my hatred and terror (it means nothing to me now to speak of terror, now that I have mocked Richard Madden, now that my throat yearns for the noose) it occurred to me that that tumultuous and doubtless happy warrior did not suspect that I possessed the Secret.
>
> (1974, p. 45. Orig. publ. in Spanish 1956)

But, I would like to stress, prolepsis can also be effectively used in so-called omniscient narration, as the following example from Muriel Spark's *The Prime of Miss Jean Brodie* shows:

> 'Speech is silver but silence is golden. Mary, are you listening? What was I saying?'
>
> Mary Macgregor, lumpy, with merely two eyes, a nose and a mouth like a snowman, who was later famous for being stupid and always to blame and who, at the age of twenty-three, lost her life in a hotel fire, ventured, 'Golden'.
>
> (1971, pp. 14–15. Orig. publ. 1961)

Like analepses, prolepses can refer either to the same character, event, or story-line figuring at that point in the text (homodiegetic) or to another character, event, or story-line (heterodiegetic). Again like analepses, they can cover either a period beyond the end of the first narrative (external), or a period anterior to it but posterior to the point at which it is narrated (internal), or combine both (mixed). In Faulkner's 'Barn Burning' the narrator describes the father's violence and then compares this quality with that of future generations:

> His father mounted to the seat where the older brother already sat and struck the gaunt mules two savage blows with the peeled willow, but

without heat. It was not even sadistic; it was exactly that same quality which in later years would cause his descendants to overrun the engine before putting a motor car into motion, striking and reigning back in the same movement.

(1971, p. 165. Orig. publ. 1939)

The comment about the future generations effects a transition from the father to other characters or another story-line and hence constitutes a heterodiegetic prolepsis in relation to the world of 'Barn Burning' (though not necessarily to that of the Faulkner saga as a whole). But since this potential story-line is posterior to the end of the first narrative (and nothing else will be said about it throughout 'Barn Burning') the prolepsis is also external.

Another external prolepsis in the same work narrates in advance what will happen twenty years later but remains attached to the boy, the object of narration preceding the prolepsis (hence the prolepsis is external but homodiegetic):

Later, twenty years later, he was to tell himself 'If I had said they wanted only truth, justice, he would have hit me again.'

(p. 167)

In all the examples given so far, the temporal shift – whether analeptic or proleptic – was effected by a narrator who is situated outside the story he narrates. Compare all the above examples with the following passage from James Joyce's 'Eveline':

She sat by the window watching the evening invade the avenue. Her head was leaned against the window curtains, and in her nostrils was the odour of dusty cretonne. She was tired.

Few people passed. The man out of the last house passed on his way home; she heard his footsteps clacking along the concrete pavement and afterwards crunching on the cinder path before the new red houses. One time there used to be a field there in which they used to play every evening with other people's children. Then a man from Belfast bought the field and built houses in it – not like their little brown houses, but bright brick houses with shining roofs. The children of the avenue used to play together in the field. . . . Now she was going to go away like the others, to leave her home. . . .

But in her new home, in a distant unknown country, it would not be like that. Then she would be married – she, Eveline. People would treat her with respect then. She would not be treated as her mother had been.

(1961, pp. 34–5. Orig. publ. 1914)

In contrast to the other examples, here the analepses and prolepses are not directly attributable to the narrator but filtered through (or, in Formalist terms, motivated by) the character's memories, fears, hopes. The status of the character-motivated anachronies is different from that of the narrator's in that they do not fully deviate from chronology. The *act* of remembering, fearing, or hoping is a part of the linear unfolding of the first narrative in 'Eveline'. It is only the *content* of the memory, fear, or hope that constitutes a past or future event. Thus, if we abstract the story from the text, such events as playing with other people's children (analepsis) or being respected in the new country (prolepsis) will probably appear twice: once as an occurrence in the past or a projected occurrence in the future, and once as a part of a present act of remembering, fearing or hoping. It is because of the present cognitive or emotional act that such events retain, at least partly, their 'normal' place in the first narrative.

DURATION

As Genette points out, the difficulty inherent in the notion of text-time is perhaps more disturbing in connection with duration than it is in connection with order and frequency. The last two can be quite easily transposed from the *time* of the story, regardless of the conventional nature of this time, to the linearity (*space*) of the text. It is not awkward to say that episode A comes after episode B in the linear disposition of the text or that episode C is told twice in the text; and such statements are quite similar to those we can make about the story: event A precedes event B in the chronology of the story; event C happens only once, etc. But it is much more difficult to describe in parallel terms the duration of the text and that of the story, for the simple reason that there is no way of measuring text-duration. The only truly temporal measure available is the time of reading and this varies from reader to reader, providing no objective standard.

For this reason, it is also more difficult to find a 'norm' against which to describe changes of duration than it was to find such a point of reference for order. For order, we remember, the 'norm' is the possibility of exact coincidence between story-time and text-time, and although text-time actually means the linear disposition in the text, one can still speak about it as 'order'. On the other hand, since no event and no textual rendering of an event can dictate an invariable reading time, there is no way of postulating an equivalence between two durations as a hypothetical 'norm'. Even a segment of pure dialogue, which has been considered by some a case of pure coincidence between story-duration and text-duration, cannot manifest complete correspondence. A dialogue can give the impression of reporting everything that was said in fact or in fiction, adding nothing to it, but even then it is incapable of rendering the rate at which the sentences were uttered or the length of the silences. It is, therefore, only by convention that one speaks of temporal equivalence of story and text in dialogue. This convention probably arises from the fact that a dialogue is a rendering of language in language, every word in the text presumably standing for a word uttered in the story, whereas the linguistic rendering of non-verbal occurrences does not seem to call for any particular fixed rate of narration.

Since it is impossible to describe the varieties of duration on the basis of an inaccessible 'norm' of identity between story and text, it is advisable to attempt a re-definition of the relations between the two 'durations' and posit a different type of 'norm' accordingly. The relations in question are, in fact, not between two 'durations' but between duration in the story (measured in minutes, hours, days, months, years) and the length of text devoted to it (in lines and pages), i.e. a temporal/spatial relationship.[8] The measure yielded by this relation in general is pace (or speed). Genette therefore proposes to use constancy of pace, rather than adequation of story and text, as the 'norm' against which to examine degrees of duration. Constancy of pace in narrative is the unchanged ratio between stoty-duration and textual length, e.g. when each year in the life of a character is treated in one page throughout the text.[9]

Taking constant pace as a 'norm', we can discern two forms of modification: acceleration and deceleration. The effect of acceleration is produced by devoting a short segment of the text to a long period of the story, relative to the 'norm' established for this text. The effect of deceleration is produced by the opposite procedure, namely devoting a long segment of the text to a short period of the story. The maximum speed is *ellipsis* (omission), where zero textual space corresponds to some story duration. In Fielding's *Tom Jones*, for example, the narrator makes a point of giving the reader 'an opportunity of employing the wonderful sagacity, of which he is master, by filling up these vacant spaces of time with his own conjectures' and then leave him 'a space of twelve years' in which to exercise his talents (1964, p. 71. Orig. publ. 1749. Quoted by Booth 1961, pp. 170–1). On the other hand, the minimum speed is manifested as a *descriptive pause*, where some segment of the text corresponds to zero story duration.[10] The description of Sulaco and its bay in Conrad's *Nostromo* (1963, pp. 17–21. Orig. publ. 1904) as well as that of Chandrapore in Forster's *A Passage to India* (1963, pp. 9–11. Orig. publ. 1924) begin the respective novels with a descriptive pause. Such a pause in the middle of the narrative can be found in the longish description of Yonville-l'Abbaye which interrupts the action in *Madame Bovary* between the Bovarys' departure toward this village and their arrival in it (1965, pp. 49–51. Orig. publ. in French 1857).

Theoretically, between these two poles there is an infinity of possible paces, but in practice these are conventionally reduced to summary and scene. In *summary*, the pace is accelerated through a textual 'condensation' or 'compression' of a given story-period into a relatively short statement of its main features. The degree of condensation can, of course, vary from summary to summary, producing multiple degrees of acceleration. Here is one example from the opening of Nabokov's *Laughter in the Dark*:

> Once upon a time there lived in Berlin, Germany, a man called Albinus. He was rich, respectable, happy; one day he abandoned his wife for the sake of a youthful mistress; he loved, was not loved; and his life ended in disaster.

> This is the whole story and we might have left it at that had there not been profit and pleasure in the telling, and although there is plenty of space on a gravestone to contain, bound in moss, the abridged version of a man's life, detail is always welcome.
>
> (1969, p. 5. Orig. publ. in Russian 1933)

A whole life is thus summed up in a few sentences, and the promised details, which are indeed always welcome, will be the expansion or deceleration constituting the bulk of the novel.

In *scene*, as was said above, story-duration and text-duration are conventionally considered identical. The purest scenic form is dialogue, like the nervous exchange between the unexpected customers and the restaurant owner in Hemingway's 'The Killers':

> 'I'll have a roast pork tenderloin with apple sauce and mashed potatoes', the first man said.
>
> 'It isn't ready yet.'
>
> 'What the hell do you put it on the card for?'
>
> 'That's the dinner', George explained. 'You can get that at six o'clock.'
>
> George looked at the clock on the wall behind the counter.
>
> 'It's five o'clock.'
>
> 'The clock says twenty minutes past five', the second man said.
>
> 'It's twenty minutes fast.'
>
> (1965, p. 57. Orig. publ. 1928)

Consisting exclusively of dialogue and a few 'stage directions', the passage looks more like a scene from a play than like a segment of a narrative. Complete novels in various periods in the history of literature were also written exclusively or almost exclusively in dialogue, e.g. Diderot's *Jacques le fataliste* (1796) and *Le neveu de Rameau* (1821) as well as several works by the Spanish author Pio Baroga.

According to some theorists (Lubbock 1921; Kayser 1948; Lämmert 1955; Ewen 1978), although dialogue is the purest form of scene, a detailed narration of an event should also be considered scenic. In this view, what characterizes a scene is the quantity of narrative information and the relative effacement of the narrator. Such is, for example, the rendering of the class's reaction to Charles Bovary's pronunciation of his name:

> A hubbub broke out, rose in *crescendo* with bursts of shrill voices (they yelled, barked, stamped, repeated Charbovari! Charbovari!), then died away into single notes, growing quieter only with great difficulty, and now and again suddenly recommencing along the line of a seat from where rose here and there, like a damp cracker going off, a stifled laugh.
>
> (1965, p. 3)

Having examined each of the four main degrees of duration separately, it may now be interesting to see an example of how a text modulates between two of them, in this case scene and summary. Flaubert's *Sentimental Education* takes some 400 pages to cover a period of roughly eleven years. This ends with a street-riot scene, which may be dated some time in 1851. In this scene Frédéric, the protagonist, sees one of his former friends being shot by a policeman who turns out to be another former friend. The quotation starts near the end of Chapter 5 of Part III:

> Then Dussardier took a step forward and started shouting:
> 'Long live the Republic!'
> He fell on his back, with his arms spread out.
> A cry of horror rose from the crowd. The policeman looked all around him, and Frédéric, open-mouthed, recognized Sénécal.
>
> VI
>
> He travelled.
> He came to know the melancholy of the steamboat, the cold awakening in the tent, the tedium of landscapes and ruins, the bitterness of interrupted friendships.
> He returned.
> He went into society, and he had other loves. But the ever-present memory of the first made them insipid; and besides, the violence of desire, the very flower of feeling, had gone. His intellectual ambitions

had also dwindled. Years went by; and he endured the idleness of his mind and the inertia of his heart.

Toward the end of March 1867, at nightfall, he was alone in his study when a woman came in.

'Madame Arnoux!'

'Frédéric!'

(1970, pp. 411–12)

In scarcely a dozen lines of text Flaubert compresses some sixteen years, before reverting to a scene pace for the narration of the renewed meeting between Frédéric and the woman he has always loved.

As in the above example, acceleration and deceleration are often evaluated by the reader as indicators of importance and centrality. Ordinarily, the more important events or conversations are given in detail (i.e. decelerated), whereas the less important ones are compressed (i.e. accelerated). But this is not always the case; sometimes the effect of shock or irony is produced by summing up briefly the most central event and rendering trivial events in detail. In Chekhov's 'Sleepy', for example, the desperate climactic act of the servant-baby-sitter, Varka, is told very briefly in a subordinate clause:

Laughing and winking and shaking her fingers at the green patch, Varka steals up to the cradle and bends over the baby. When she has strangled him, she quickly lies down on the floor, laughs with delight that she can sleep, and in a minute is sleeping as sound as the dead.

(1927, p. 147. Orig. publ. in Russian 1888)

Even more extreme is Kleist's 'The Marquise of O-' (1962, pp. 39–90. Orig. publ. in German, 1806) where the most crucial moment in the story is elided in the text. Whereas later indications make it probable that during that moment the unconscious Marquise of O- was raped by the Count F-, the text coyly avoids confirming this inference to the very end. In this example, ellipsis in duration clearly coincides with a permanent information gap (see chapter 9).

FREQUENCY

Frequency, a temporal component not treated in narrative theory before Genette, is the relation between the number of times an event appears in the story and the number of times it is narrated (or mentioned) in the text. Frequency, then, involves repetition, and repetition is a mental construct attained by an elimination of the specific qualities of each occurrence and a preservation of only those qualities which it shares with similar occurrences. Strictly speaking, no event is repeatable in all respects, nor is a repeated segment of the text quite the same, since its new location puts it in a different context which necessarily changes its meaning. This paradox is developed by Borges in 'Pierre Menard, Author of the *Quixote*' (1974. Orig. publ. in Spanish 1956). In this text, ostensibly an obituary article on a little known French symbolist writer, we are informed that his most ambitious literary project consisted in writing again *Don Quixote*. Before his untimely death Pierre Menard managed to produce only Chapters 9, 38 and a fragment of Chapter 22, all identical in every word to the corresponding portions of Cervantes's text (orig. publ. in Spanish 1605–1616). As the fictional narrator comments, the very same text coming from a French Decadent esthete and from a retired Spanish soldier takes a completely different sense, the former gaining in richness from the intervening changes in history and culture.

Considered as mental constructs, repetition-relations between story events and their narration in the text can take the following forms:

Singulative, i.e. telling once what 'happened' once. This is the most common narrative form, and examples are therefore unnecessary. To the same category belongs the less common phenomenon of narrating n times what 'happened' n times, since here too each mention in the text corresponds to one occurrence in the story. This practice is parodied in *Don Quixote* when Sancho tells the story of a fisherman who had to transport three hundred goats in a boat that had room only for one. As Sancho narrates, it becomes clear that he intends to tell the event three hundred times, corresponding to the number of journeys the fisherman undertook. Quixote impatiently comments: 'Take it that they are all across . . . and do not go on coming and going like that, or you will never get them all over in a year' (1950, p. 154). From a theoretical point of view, however, the more common practice of telling once what 'happened' once may be seen as a specific instance of the more inclusive type 'telling n times what happened n times' (and 'n' here equals 1).

Repetitive, i.e. telling n times what 'happened' once. Thus, the main event in Faulkner's Absalom, Absalom! (1936), the murder of Charles Bon by Henry Sutpen, is narrated thirty-nine times, sometimes with, sometimes without changes of narrator, focalizer, duration, narrative subject, style, etc. (Rimmon-Kenan, forthcoming).

Iterative, i.e. telling once what 'happened' n times. Such is the opening of Lawrence's The Rainbow, narrating in one time the recurrent activities of the Brangwen men over the years:

> Their life and interrelations were such, feeling the pulse and the body of the soil, that opened to their furrow for the grain, and became smooth and supple after their ploughing, and clung to their feet with a weight that pulled like desire, lying and responsive when the crops were shorn away. . . . They took the udder of the cows, the cows yielded milk and pulse against the hands of the men, the pulse of the blood of the teats of the cows beat into the pulse of the hands of the men.
>
> (1973, p. 8. Orig. publ. 1915)

The passage is clearly iterative, prefiguring thereby the cyclic nature of the relationship between the generations and within each generation.[11]

It has often been suggested that one of the characteristics of modern narratives is the subversive treatment of the various categories of time. While this seems to me basically true (with many exceptions, of course), it does not invalidate the categories presented here. On the contrary, subversion can only be conceived of against the background of (or even within) a network of possibilities, such as this chapter has attempted to outline. Moreover, while the treatment of time may undergo various changes, time itself is indispensible to both story and text. To eliminate it (if this were possible) would be to eliminate all narrative fiction.

5

TEXT: CHARACTERIZATION

Character, as one construct within the abstracted story, can be described in terms of a network of character-traits. These traits, however, may or may not appear as such in the text. How, then, is the construct arrived at? By assembling various character-indicators distributed along the text-continuum and, when necessary, inferring the traits from them. It is these indicators that I seek to define under the heading of 'characterization'.

In principle, any element in the text may serve as an indicator of character and, conversely, character-indicators may serve other purposes as well (see the point about the reversibility of hierarchies in chapter 3, p. 36). But there are elements which are most frequently, though not exclusively, associated with characterization, and these are the subject of the present chapter. In the study of particular texts, it should be remembered that the same means of characterization may be used differently by different authors or in different works by the same author and sometimes even within the same work. However, in this general presentation of characterization such differences cannot be explored.

There are two basic types of textual indicators of character: direct definition and indirect presentation (Ewen 1971; 1980, pp. 47–8).[1] The first type names the trait by an adjective (e.g. 'he was good-hearted'), an abstract noun ('his goodness knew no bounds'), or possibly some other kind of noun ('she was a real bitch') or part of speech ('he loves only himself'). The second type, on the other hand, does not mention the trait but displays and exemplifies it in various ways, leaving to the reader the task of inferring the quality they imply.

DIRECT DEFINITION

'Isabel Archer was a young person of many theories; her imagination was remarkably active. . . . Her thoughts were a tangle of vague out-lines . . .' – this is how Henry James's narrator defines some prominent traits of the heroine of The Portrait of a Lady (1966, p. 49. Orig. publ. 1881). Such naming of a character's qualities counts as direct charac-terization only if it proceeds from the most authoritative voice in the text (on 'voices' see chapter 7, pp. 86–9, 94–103). Had the same words been spoken by the people of Albany, for example, they would probably have carried less weight, serving reflexively to characterize them as much as (if not more than) Isabel. If narrow-minded, dull characters call someone 'a person of many theories' or consider that character's imagination 'remarkably active', their views need not be taken as a reliable affirmation of these qualities in a character whose exceptionality may be only in the eyes of mediocre beholders. The beholders' comments may thus be an indication of their own distrust of theories or paucity of imagination rather than a trustworthy definition of the character they discuss. But when these exceptional qualities are attributed to Isabel by an authoritative narrator, the reader is implicitly called upon to accept the definitions.[2]

Definition is akin to generalization and conceptualization. It is also both explicit and supra-temporal. Consequently, its dominance in a given text is liable to produce a rational, authoritative and static impression. This impression may be alleviated if the definitions seem to emerge gradually from concrete details, or are immediately exemplified by specific behaviour, or presented together with other means of characterization. In the early period of the novel, roughly until the end of the last century, when the human personality was grasped as a combination of qualities shared by many people, the generalizing, classificatory nature of definition was considered an asset.

Its explicitness and 'closed' effect did not disturb a literature where these qualities manifested themselves in many other ways as well. The economical character of definition and its capacity to guide the reader's response recommended it to traditional novelists. On the other hand, in an individualistic and relativistic period like our own, generalization and classification are less easily tolerated, and the economy of definition is grasped as reductive. Moreover, in the present day, when suggestiveness and indeterminacy are preferred to closure and definitiveness and when emphasis is put on the active role of the reader, the explicitness and guiding capacity of direct definition are often considered drawbacks rather than advantages. As a result, definition is less frequently used in twentieth-century fiction and indirect presentation tends to predominate (Ewen 1980, pp. 51–2).

INDIRECT PRESENTATION

A presentation is indirect when rather than mentioning a trait, it displays and exemplifies it in various ways. Some of these ways will be enumerated in the following discussion.

Action

A trait may be implied both by one-time (or non-routine) actions, like Meursault's murder of the Arab in Camus's *L'Etranger* (1942), and by habitual ones, like Eveline's dusting of the house in Joyce's short story bearing her name (1914). One-time actions tend to evoke the dynamic aspect of the character, often playing a part in a turning point in the narrative. By contrast, habitual actions tend to reveal the character's unchanging or static aspect, often having a comic or ironic effect, as when a character clings to old habits in a situation which renders them inadequate. Although a one-time action does not reflect *constant* qualities, it is not less characteristic of the character. On the contrary, its dramatic impact often suggests that the traits it reveals are qualitatively more crucial than the numerous habits which represent the character's routine.

Both one-time and habitual actions can belong to one of the following categories: act of commission (i.e. something performed by the character), act of omission (something which the character should, but does not do), and contemplated act (an unrealized plan or intention of the character).[3] Meursault's (one-time) murder and Eveline's (habitual) dusting are both acts of commission. For a crucial one-time act of omission we can turn to another novel by Camus, *La Chute* (1956). In it, the failure of the character-narrator to jump into the river and save the drowning woman remains an obsession to him and a central concern in the text. Habitual omissions characterize Faulkner's Emily (1930), as when she repeatedly neglects to pay her municipal taxes. A contemplated act may both imply a latent trait and suggest possible reasons for its remaining latent, as in the following passage from Spark's *The Prime of Miss Jean Brodie:*

> Then suddenly Sandy wanted to be kind to Mary Macgregor, and thought of possibilities of feeling nice from being nice to Mary instead of blaming her. . . . The sound of Miss Brodie's presence, just when it was on the tip of Sandy's tongue to be nice to Mary Macgregor, arrested the urge.
>
> (1971, p. 30. Orig. publ. 1961)

Sandy's latent propensity to be kind as well as its erasure under Miss Brodie's influence can be glimpsed in this contemplated act. When contemplated acts become habitual, the character's passivity or shrinking from action may be implied. Hamlet, of course, has become the proverbial prototype of this characteristic.

All these kinds of action can (but need not) be endowed with a symbolic dimension. Two examples will suffice. Shortly before the first love scene between Connie Chatterley and the gamekeeper in Lawrence's novel, the two come across a hen and a chick:

> 'There!' he said, holding out his hand to her. She took the little drab thing between her hands, and there it stood. . . . But it lifted its handsome clean-shaped little head boldly, and looked sharply round, and gave a little 'peep'. 'So adorable! So cheeky!' she said softly.
> The keeper, squatting beside her, was also watching with an amused face the bold little bird in her hands. Suddenly he saw a tear fall on her wrist.

> ... She was kneeling and holding her two hands slowly forward, blindly, so that the chicken should run in to the mother-hen again. . . . He came quickly toward her and crouched beside her again, taking the chick from her hands, because she was afraid of the hen, and putting it back in the coop. . . . Her face was averted and she was crying blindly.
>
> (1961, p. 119. Orig. publ. 1928)

Connie's behaviour in this scene symbolizes her yearning for warmth, love and maternity, all absent in her marriage.

Whereas in the passage from Lawrence the symbolism lies in acts of commission (taking the chick between the hands, gently guiding it toward the mother-hen, crying), the second example, again taken from *The Portrait of a Lady*, confers symbolic significance on an act of omission:

> She [Isabel] knew that this silent, motionless portal opened into the street; if the sidelights had not been filled with green paper she might have looked out upon the little brown stoop and the well-worn brick pavement. But she had no wish to look out, for this would have interfered with her theory that there was a strange, unseen place on the other side – a place which became to the child's imagination, according to its different moods, a region of delight or of terror. . . . She had never opened the bolted door nor removed the green paper (renewed by other hands) from its sidelights; she had never assured herself that the vulgar street lay beyond.
>
> (1966, p. 25)

Isabel's not opening the door to the street symbolically suggests her preference for illusion over reality, a characteristic which will later play an important part in her tragic career.

Speech

A character's speech, whether in conversation or as a silent activity of the mind, can be indicative of a trait or traits both through its content and through its form. It is mainly the content of Jason's statement in Faulkner's *The Sound and the Fury* that suggests his bigotry:

'I give every man his due, regardless of religion or anything else. I have nothing against Jews as an individual', I says, 'It's just the race.'

(1965, p. 173. Orig. publ. 1931)

But the inner contradiction (he gives people their due *regardless* of religion, yet dislikes the Jews *as* a race) and the underlying cliché ('some of my best friends are Jews' or some similar expression) clearly play a part in stressing the specious logic characteristic of his (or any) bigotry. Similarly, what one character says about another may characterize not only the one spoken about but also the one who speaks (see p. 60).

The form or style of speech is a common means of characterization in texts where the characters' language is individuated and distinguished from that of the narrator. Style may be indicative of origin, dwelling place, social class, or profession. Thus the stereotypic traits of a Jew and a rabbi are evoked by the Hebrew and Yiddish expressions as well as by the turn of phrases in the following passage from Bellow's *Herzog*:

'And she took hold of . . .'
'of what? *Beged*'
'*Beged*. A coat'
'A garment, you little thief. *Mamzer*! I'm sorry for your father. Some heir he's got! Some *kaddish*! Ham and pork you'll be eating, before his body is in the grave. And you, Herzog, with those behemoth eyes – *V'yaizov bigdo b'yodo?*'
'And he left it in her hands'
'Left what?'
'*Bigdo*, the garment'
'You watch your step, Herzog, Moses. Your mother thinks you'll be a great *lamden* – a rabbi. But I know you, how lazy you are. Mothers' hearts are broken by *mamzeirim* like you! Eh! do I know you, Herzog? Through and through.'

(1973, pp. 137–8. Orig. publ. 1964)

In addition to the social aspect of a character revealed by his style, individual characteristics can also be suggested by it. Thus the abun-

dance of subordinate clauses and the recurrent qualification of statements in the language of many of Henry James's characters implies
their tendency to follow all the nuances of a thought or feeling as well
as the painstaking quality of their intellect.

Action and speech convey character-traits through a cause and effect
relation which the reader deciphers 'in reverse': X killed the dragon,
'therefore' he is brave; Y uses many foreign words, 'therefore' she is a
snob.[4] But indirect presentation may also rely on a relation of spatial
contiguity. This is the case of external appearance and environment. A
causal connection may, in fact, be present, though not dominant, here
too, as when a character's shabby dress or dirty room not only connote
his state of depression but also result from it. Another difference
between the two kinds of indirect indicators is that the first is located in
time whereas the second is non-temporal. Again, the difference is not
absolute, for a description of a character's external appearance or
environment may refer to a specific point in time ('on that day she
wore a black coat' etc.). However, such time-bound descriptions tend
to characterize a transitory mood rather than a 'relatively stable or
abiding personal quality' which is Chatman's definition of a character
trait (1978, p. 127).

External appearance

Ever since the beginning of narrative fiction, external appearance was
used to imply character-traits, but only under the influence of Lavater, a
Swiss philosopher and theologian (1741–1801), and his theory of
physiognomy has the connection between the two acquired a pseudo-
scientific status. Lavater analysed portraits of various historical figures
as well as people of his own time (see example in Ewen 1980, pp. 57–8)
in order to demonstrate the necessary and direct connection between
facial features and personality traits. The impact of his theory on Balzac
and other nineteenth-century authors was great indeed. But even in
our century, when the scientific validity of Lavater's theory has been
completely discredited, the metonymic relation between external
appearance and character-traits has remained a powerful resource in
the hand of many writers. One should distinguish in this connection
between those external features which are grasped as beyond the

character's control, such as height, colour of eyes, length of nose (features which get scarcer with the advancement of modern cosmetics and plastic surgery) and those which at least partly depend on him, like hair-style and clothes. While the first group characterizes through contiguity alone, the second has additional causal overtones (Ewen 1980, p. 59). Both kinds can be found in the description of Laura, the heroine of Porter's 'Flowering Judas', and both suggest her repression of warmth, sexuality and *joie de vivre*:

> (a) . . . but all praise her gray eyes, and the soft, round under lip which promises gayety, yet is always grave, nearly always firmly closed.
>
> (1971, p. 389. Orig. publ. 1930)

> (b) . . . this simple girl who covers her great round breasts with thick dark cloth, and who hides long, invaluably beautiful legs under a heavy skirt. She is almost thin except for the incomprehensible fullness of her breasts, like a nursing mother's . . . .
>
> (1971, p. 392)

At times the external description speaks for itself; at other times its relation to a trait is explicated by the narrator, e.g. 'his brown eyes expressed sadness and innocence'. Such explanations may function as disguised definitions rather than as indirect characterization. This happens when a non-visual quality is attributed – as in a synecdoche – to one part of the character's physique rather than to the character as a whole (e.g. 'her intelligent eyes' instead of 'she is intelligent'). Ewen calls these 'seeming descriptions' and distinguishes them from the kind of external appearance discussed so far (1980, p. 61).

Environment

A character's physical surrounding (room, house, street, town) as well as his human environment (family, social class) are also often used as trait-connoting metonymies. As with external appearance, the relation of contiguity is frequently supplemented by that of causality. Miss Emily's dilapidated house, with its clouds of dust and its dank smell, is a metonymy of her decadence, but its decay is also a result of her poverty and her morbid temperament. Again as with external appearance, a pseudo-scientific connection between character and environment was established in the nineteenth century. The doctrine of race, moment and milieu, expounded by the French historian and philosopher Hippolyte Taine (1828–1893) had a decisive influence on the use of environment in the writing of Balzac and Zola. However, the causality postulated by this doctrine is less marked in Balzac's use of spatial metonymies than in Zola's. This difference may be illustrated by a detailed comparison (which I cannot undertake here) of, say, the description of the Maison Vauquer and its inhabitants in *Le Père Goriot* (1834) and that of the mine and its workers in *Germinal* (1885).

REINFORCEMENT BY ANALOGY

I treat analogy as a reinforcement of characterization rather than as a separate type of character-indicator (equivalent to direct definition and indirect presentation) because its characterizing capacity depends on the prior establishment, by other means, of the traits on which it is based. A grey and dreary landscape, for example, is not likely to imply itself a character's pessimism, but it may enhance the reader's perception of this trait once it has been revealed through the character's action, speech or external appearance.[5]

The differentiation between analogy and other indicators of character should be carried a bit further. Since metaphoric (analogous) elements tend to be implicit in metonymies, one may question the distinction between what I call analogy and such forms of metonymic presentation as external appearance and environment. Does not the rigidity of Laura's dress parallel that of her personality, and is not the decay of Miss Emily's house analogous to her own decline? The answer to both questions is Yes, and yet these indirect presentations are based mainly on contiguity, a relation either absent from or much less dominant in the analogies discussed here. Moreover, as we have seen above, indirect presentation often involves an implicit story-causality. Analogy, on the other hand, is a purely textual link, independent of story-causality. As Ewen points out, many – though not all – analogies may have developed out of conceptions involving causality, like the medieval belief in the cause and effect relations between disorder in the human world and upheaval in nature, but they are grasped as purely analogous characterization when the causal connection is no longer strongly operative (1980, p. 100). Although the transition from one type to the other is neither abrupt nor neat and the two may often overlap in practice, the distinction is still valid in principle.

Three ways in which analogy can reinforce characterization will be discussed below, without presuming that they are exhaustive. In all three, the analogy may emphasize either the similarity or the contrast between the two elements compared, and it may be either explicitly stated in the text or implicity left for the reader to discover.

Analogous names

According to Hamon (1977, pp. 147–50. Orig. publ. 1972), names can parallel character-traits in four ways: (1) Visual, as when the letter O is associated with a round and fat character and the letter I with a tall thin one (his example). (2) Acoustic, whether in onomatopoeia, like the buzz of flies in the name 'Beelzebub', or in less strictly onomato-poeic form, like 'Akaky Akakievitch' in Gogol's 'The Overcoat' (1842), ridiculed by the very sound of his name. (3) Articulatory, like Dick-ens's 'Grad-grind' in Hard Times (1854), suggesting the main quality of the character by the mouthing of the name and the muscle activity it requires. (4) Morphological, like the presence of 'boeuf' (bull) in 'Bov/ary' or the combination of 'hors' + 'la' (out + there) in the name of Maupassant's mysterious creature, le Horla (1887).

Close to Hamon's last category, though not necessarily based on morphological combinations are the semantic connections which Ewen discusses (1980, pp. 102–7). In allegories, the name represents the main trait(s) of a character: Pride, Lust, Goodman. (An interesting contemporary usage of this is to be found in Zinoviev's The Yawning Heights (1976) which castigates Soviet society in a flood of brief sketches of such stereotypes as 'Careerist', 'Slanderer', 'Chatterer', 'Sociologist' and at last 'Truth-teller'. But even non-allegorical texts often have recourse to a semantic parallelism between name and trait. Mrs Newsome in James's The Ambassadors (1903) represents the new world, the betrayer in Spark's The Prime of Miss Jean Brodie is called 'Sandy

Stranger', and the self-effacing beauty who gave her name to Maupassant's story is named 'Mademoiselle Perle' (1886). Sometimes the analogy is based on literary or mythological allusions, as in the name 'Daedalus' in Joyce's *A Portrait of the Artist* (1916), transferring to Stephen the creativity, pride and possibility of fall associated with his Greek ancestor.

Rather than stressing similarity, analogy can also emphasize contrast between name and trait, frequently creating an ironic effect. This is the case when Razumov, son of reason (from a Polish root), is shown in Conrad's *Under Western Eyes* (1911) to be governed by unconscious motives much more frequently than by reason, often precisely when he prides himself on his rationality. Like similarities, contrasts can also be underscored by literary allusions. When the name Laura, borrowed from the glorified beloved of Petrarch's sonnets, is bestowed on a love-denying revolutionist in Porter's 'Flowering Judas', the result is a clash which ironically underscores the perversion involved in Laura's asceticism. Although 'Ulysses' is not the name of the main character in Joyce's novel (1922), its title-position suggests an analogy with the main character, Bloom, and the contrast between the mythological hero and his modern counterpart sheds ironic light on the latter.

Analogous landscape

As we have seen (pp. 66–7), the physical or social environment of a character does not only present a trait or traits indirectly but, being man-made, may also cause it or be caused by it (x lives in a very poor neighbourhood, therefore he is cheerless, or – the other way round – Y is depressed, therefore his house is neglected). Landscape, on the other hand, is independent of man, and hence does not normally entertain a relation of story-causality with the characters (although a character's choice to live or pass his time in a certain natural location may suggest a cause-and-effect relation). The analogy established by the text between a certain landscape and a character-trait may be either 'straight' (based on similarity) or 'inverse' (emphasizing contrast). Catherine and Heathcliff in Bronte's *Wuthering Heights* (1847) are similar to the wilderness in which they live, just as the nature of the

Linton family parallels the peacefulness of their dwelling place. On the other hand, in Bialik's narrative poem, 'In the City of Slaughter' (1904), the cruelty of the killers (as well as the indifference of God) is emphasized by the sharp contrast between the *pogrom* and the idyllic landscape in which it takes place: 'The sun shone, the acacia bloomed, and the slaughterer hacked' (my own literal translation). Landscape can be analogous not only to a character-trait but also to a passing mood; however in this capacity it is not strictly a character-indicator.

Analogy between characters

When two characters are presented in similar circumstances, the similarity or contrast between their behaviour emphasizes traits characteristic of both. Thus there is reciprocal characterization in the contrasted behaviour of Dostoevsky's four brothers Karamazov toward their father (1880). Similarly, in Shakespeare's *King Lear* the sisters' cruelty underscores Cordelia's goodness (and vice-versa) by way of contrast, but the analogy also suggests a similarity between the evil and the good sisters: while, in the opening scene, Regan and Goneril disguise the truth by overstatement, Cordelia disguises it by understatement.

Having mapped the main general categories pertaining to characterization, it seems appropriate to conclude with a few considerations deriving from the study of individual texts. First, a character indicator does not always suggest one trait to the exclusion of others; it may imply the co-presence of several traits, or cause the reader to hesitate among various labels. Second, an enumeration of means of characterization used in individual texts is insufficient. It may be instructive, for example, to establish which type of characterization predominates in a given text or for a given character. This can then be related, according to the interests of the critic, to the kind of character in question, the thematic concern(s) of the work, the genre to which it belongs, the preferences of the author, the norms of the period, and the like. Equally interesting is an examination of the interaction among the various means of characterization. The result, as well as the reading process, will be different according to whether the indicators repeat the same trait in different ways, complement each other, partially overlap, or conflict with each other (Ewen 1971, p. 24). Such an analysis is bound to yield complexities and nuances far beyond what could be presented here.

6

TEXT: FOCALIZATION

FOCALIZATION AND/VERSUS NARRATION

The story is presented in the text through the mediation of some 'prism', 'perspective', 'angle of vision', verbalized by the narrator though not necessarily his. Following Genette (1972), I call this mediation 'focalization'. However, since Anglo-American readers are likely to associate 'prism', 'perspective', or 'angle of vision' with the more common term 'point of view', I shall begin by explaining why I substitute 'focalization' for it.

Genette considers 'focalization' to have a degree of abstractness which avoids the specifically visual connotations of 'point of view' as well as of the equivalent French terms, 'vision' (Pouillon 1946) or 'champ' (as in Blin's 'restrictions de champ', 1954) (Genette 1972, p. 206).[1] It seems to me, however, that the term 'focalization' is not free of optical-photographic connotations, and – like 'point of view' – its purely visual sense has to be broadened to include cognitive, emotive and ideological orientation (see pp. 79–82). My own reason for choosing 'focalization' is different from Genette's, although it resides precisely in his treatment of it as a technical term. Genette's treatment has the great advantage of dispelling the confusion between perspective and narration which often occurs when 'point of view' or similar terms are used.

As Genette has shown, most studies of point of view (e.g. Brooks and Warren 1959. Orig. publ. 1943; Stanzel 1955; Friedman 1955; Booth 1961; Romberg 1962) treat two related but different questions as if they were interchangeable. Briefly formulated, these questions are 'who sees?' v. 'who speaks?' Obviously, a person (and, by analogy, a narrative agent)[2] is capable of both speaking and seeing, and even of doing both things at the same time – a state of affairs which facilitates the confusion between the two activities. Moreover, it is almost impossible to speak without betraying some personal 'point of view', if only through the very language used. But a person (and, by analogy, a narrative agent) is also capable of undertaking to tell what another person sees or has seen. Thus, speaking and seeing, narration and focalization, may, but need not, be attributed to the same agent. The distinction between the two activities is a theoretical necessity, and only on its basis can the interrelations between them be studied with precision.

Specific examples will, I hope, make clear both the reasons for the confusion and the implications of the distinction. It is generally agreed that in Joyce's *A Portrait of the Artist* almost everything is seen through Stephen's eyes. According to Booth, 'any sustained inside view, of whatever depth, temporarily turns the character whose mind is shown into a narrator' (1961, p. 164). If this is accepted, Stephen becomes not only a vehicle of focalization (a 'focalizer') but also a narrator.[3] However, even in passages where the language gets as close as possible to a 'translation' of Stephen's perceptions, verbal communication and non-verbal focalization remain separate. Take, for example, the opening of the novel:

> Once upon a time and a very good time it was there was a moocow coming down along the road and this moocow that was coming down along the road met a nicens little boy named baby tuckoo. . . .
>
> His father told him that story: his father looked at him through a glass: he had a hairy face.
>
> He was baby tuckoo. The moocow came down the road where Betty Byrne lived: she sold lemon platt.
>
> (1963, p. 7. Orig. publ. 1916)

The language not only conveys the perceptions of the child, it also contains childish expressions. Yet it is not Stephen's language, nor is Stephen the narrator in this passage. For one thing, a baby who still wets the bed (see the next paragraph in the novel) is incapable of formulating complete sentences like those quoted above. For another, in this passage Stephen is referred to in the third person ('he', 'him'), an unlikely procedure if he himself were the narrator of his story (although one could perhaps argue that children often do this).

Similarly, focalization and narration are separate in so-called first-person retrospective narratives, although this is usually ignored by studies of point of view.[4] Pip, in Dickens's *Great Expectations*, narrates events that happened to him in the past:

> 'You are to wait here, you boy', said Estella and disappeared and closed the door.
> I took the opportunity of being alone in the court-yard, to look at my coarse hands and my common boots. My opinion of those accessories was not favourable. They had never troubled me before, but they troubled me now, as vulgar appendages.
>
> (1978, pp. 91–2. Orig. publ. 1860/61)

Although this is a record of things as the child saw, felt, understood them, words like 'accessories' and 'appendages' are clearly not within a child's vocabulary. The narrator is Pip, the adult, while the focalizer is Pip, the child.[5]

The implications of the foregoing discussion can now be formulated explicitly:

1   In principle, focalization and narration are distinct activities.
2   In so-called 'third-person centre of consciousness' (James's *The Ambassadors*, Joyce's *Portrait*), the centre of consciousness (or 'reflector') is the focalizer, while the user of the third person is the narrator.
3   Focalization and narration are also separate in first-person retrospective narratives.
4   As far as focalization is concerned, there is no difference between third-person centre of consciousness and first-person retrospective

narration. In both, the focalizer is a character within the represented world. The only difference between the two is the identity of the narrator.

5 However, focalization and narration may sometimes be combined, as will be shown in the next section.

So far I have discussed focalization and its vehicle, the focalizer. Narratives, however, are not only focalized *by* someone but also *on* someone or something (Bal 1977, p. 29). In other words, focalization has both a subject and an object. The subject (the 'focalizer') is the agent whose perception orients the presentation, whereas the object (the 'focalized') is what the focalizer perceives (Bal 1977, p. 33). Both focalizer and focalized will be taken into account in the following classification.

TYPES OF FOCALIZATION

Two criteria will be used in this section to discuss the different types of focalization: position relative to the story, and degree of persistence. The categories established here will be more fully treated in the next section, where their specific manifestations in different facets of focalization will be discussed.

Position relative to the story

Focalization can be either external or internal to the story.[6] External focalization is felt to be close to the narrating agent, and its vehicle is therefore called 'narrator-focalizer' (Bal 1977, p. 37). This is the type of focalization predominant in Fielding's *Tom Jones* (1749), Balzac's *Le Père Goriot* (1834), and Forster's *A Passage to India* (1924), to mention only a few texts. But external focalization can also occur in first person narratives, either when the temporal and psychological distance between narrator and character is minimal (as in Camus's *L'Etranger*, 1957) or when the perception through which the story is rendered is that of the narrating self rather than that of the experiencing self. An interesting, problematic example is Joyce's 'Araby' (1914) which will be discussed below (pp. 83–5).

As the term suggests, the locus of internal focalization is inside the represented events. This type generally takes the form of a character-focalizer, like little Sartoris Snopes in Faulkner's 'Barn Burning' (1939) or Pip the child in many parts of *Great Expectations*. But internal focalization is sometimes no more than a textual stance, although even such an unpersonified stance tends to be endowed by readers with the qualities of a character. Here is a classic example from Robbe-Grillet's *Jealousy*:

Now A . . . has come into the bedroom by the inside door opening onto the central hallway. She does not look at the wide open window through which – from the door – she would see this corner of the terrace. Now she has turned back toward the door to close it behind her. . . .

The heavy hand-rail of the balustrade has almost no point left on top. The gray of the wood shows through, streaked with tiny longitudinal cracks. On the other side of this rail, a good six feet below the level of the veranda, the garden begins.

But from the far side of the bedroom the eye carries over the balustrade and touches ground only much further away, on the opposite slope of the little valley, among the banana trees of the plantation. The sun cannot be seen between their thick clusters of wide green leaves. However, since this sector has been under cultivation only recently, the regular criss-crossing of the rows of trees can still be clearly followed. The same is true of almost all the property visible from here. . . .

(1965, pp. 39–40. Orig. publ. in French 1957)

There is no personified focalizer here (or anywhere else in *Jealousy*), and at first sight the focalization may seem external. However, expressions like 'she would see *this* corner', 'from the far side of the bedroom *the eye* carries over the balustrade', 'the property visible from *here*' imply a position within the story from which things are observed. Morrissette (1963) was the first to conjecture – as many readers after him have done – that 'the eye' is that of the jealous husband whose vision 'colours' the information conveyed in the text.

One test for distinguishing between external and internal focalization is the attempt to 'rewrite' the given segment in the first person. If this is feasible – the segment is internally focalized, if not – the focalization is external (Barthes 1966, p. 20; Genette 1972, p. 210). However, it is not clear whether this feasibility can be defined in strictly grammatical terms or in the much more elusive terms of verisimilitude.

Just as the focalizer can be external or internal to the represented events, so the focalized can be seen either from without or from within.[7] However, the two parallel classifications do not necessarily coincide (which is why I choose 'external/internal' for one and 'without/within' for the other). An external focalizer may perceive an object either from without or from within. In the first case, only the outward manifestations of the object (person or thing) are presented, as in many Biblical narratives:

> And Abraham rose up early in the morning, and saddled his ass, and took two of his young men with him, and Isaac his son, and clave the wood for the burnt offering, and rose up, and went unto the place which God had told him.
>
> (Genesis 22: 3)

Abraham is about to sacrifice his son, yet only his external actions are presented, his feelings and thoughts remaining opaque. In the second case, the external focalizer (narrator-focalizer) presents the focalized from within, penetrating his feelings and thoughts. This is what happens in the following passage from Lawrence's *Sons and Lovers*:

> She [Miriam] did not at bottom believe she ever would have him. She did not believe in herself primarily; doubted whether she could ever be what he would demand of her. Certainly she never saw herself living happily through a lifetime with him. She saw tragedy, sorrow and sacrifice ahead. And in sacrifice she was proud, in renunciation she was strong, for she did not trust herself to support everyday life. She was prepared for the big things and the deep things, like tragedy. It was the sufficiency of the small day-life she could not trust.
>
> (1962, p. 265. Orig. publ. 1913)

Similarly, an internal focalizer may perceive the object from within, especially when she herself is both focalizer and focalized, like Molly Bloom in Joyce's *Ulysses* (1922), but his or her perception may also be confined to the outward manifestations of the focalized, as in the passage quoted from *Jealousy* and in many narratives by Kafka and Hemingway.

Degree of persistence

Focalization may remain fixed throughout the narrative, as in James's *What Maisie Knew* (1897), but it can also alternate between two predominant focalizers, as in White's *The Solid Mandala* (1966), or shift among several, as in Faulkner's *The Sound and the Fury* (1931). This distinction between fixed, variable and multiple focalization applies to the focalized no less than to the focalizer.

FACETS OF FOCALIZATION

In the beginning of this chapter, I stated that the purely visual sense of 'focalization' is too narrow. The time has come to discuss the various facets of the phenomenon and to show how the external/internal criterion manifests itself in each. The degree of persistence will be taken up when relevant.[8]

The perceptual facet

Perception (sight, hearing, smell, etc.) is determined by two main coordinates: space and time.

Space

'Translated' into spatial terms the external/internal position of the focalizer takes the form of a bird's-eye view v. that of a limited observer. In the first, the focalizer is located at a point far above the object(s) of his perception. This is the classical position of a narrator-focalizer, yielding either a panoramic view or a 'simultaneous' focalization of things 'happening' in different places. Panoramic views are frequent in the beginning or end of a narrative or of one of its scenes (Uspensky 1973, p. 64).[9] Such is the description of Sulaco in the beginning of Conrad's *Nostromo* (1904) and that of Chandrapore in the opening of

Forster's *A Passage to India* (1924). Simultaneous focalization can be conveniently exemplified by White's *Voss* (1960. Orig. publ. 1957). While Voss himself is struggling to cross the Australian desert, the reader is given a glimpse of the woman he left behind in Sydney (1960, p. 394). Later, the last survivor of the expedition just manages to reach a rocky outcrop, where he collapses. A simultaneous focalization suggests that the leader of the rescue party is gazing at the same 'inhospitable rocks in the near distance' (p. 427) when he announces his decision to return to the coast and abandon the search for the missing expedition.

A panoramic or simultaneous view is impossible when focalization is attached to a character or to an unpersonified position internal to the story. In such cases, if the character-focalizer is inside a locked room, the room itself can be presented through his eyes, but not the street, unless there is a window through which he looks out (as in Joyce's 'Eveline', 1914). If the internal focalizer later goes out into the street, the reader may be brought along. This limitation explains why the inside of Miss Emily's house in Faulkner's 'A Rose for Emily' (1930) is described only when focalized by the tax delegation and then again at the end, after her death. Since the whole text is internally focalized by one of the townspeople, and since nobody was given permission to enter Emily's house for years, the internal focalizer can only perceive the interior if he 'accompanies' the intruders.

Spatial focalization may change from a bird's-eye view to that of a limited observer or from the view of one limited observer to that of another. Thus in *War and Peace* (1864–69), the reader 'accompanies' Pierre to the battle of Borodino, but does not remain attached to Pierre's perceptions throughout the battle. 'Having reached the battlefield we are not necessarily bound to him; we may leave him and assume different spatial positions' (Uspensky 1973, pp. 58–9).

Time

External focalization is panchronic in the case of an unpersonified focalizer, and retrospective in the case of a character focalizing his own past. On the other hand, internal focalization is synchronous with the information regulated by the focalizer. In other words, an external focalizer has at his disposal all the temporal dimensions of the story (past, present and future), whereas an internal focalizer is limited to the 'present'. of the characters (Uspensky 1973, pp. 67, 113). 'A Rose for Emily' is again a useful example. The narrator and the focalizer in this narrative are the same 'person': an inhabitant of Emily's town. However, the temporal position of the two vis-à-vis the narrated events shows them to be separate agents. The narrator is temporally external to the story, knowing the end when he starts the narration. Yet he chooses not to divulge his retrospective understanding, limiting his perceptions to those of the townspeople at the time of the events. The focalizer is thus not the citizen as narrator but the townspeople (including himself) as limited observers at an earlier stage. This choice of an internal focalizer lends plausibility to the withholding of information used to create the shock effect when the discovery of Homer's corpse is narrated.

The psychological facet

Whereas the perceptual facet has to do with the focalizer's sensory range, the psychological facet concerns his mind and emotions.[10] As the previous sentence suggests, the determining components are again two: the cognitive and the emotive orientation of the focalizer towards the focalized.

The cognitive component

Knowledge, conjecture, belief; memory – these are some of the terms of cognition. Conceived of in these terms, the opposition between external and internal focalization becomes that between unrestricted and restricted knowledge. In principle, the external focalizer (or narrator-focalizer) knows everything about the represented world, and when he restricts his knowledge, he does so out of rhetorical considerations (like the attempt to create an effect of surprise and shock in 'A Rose for Emily'). The knowledge of an internal focalizer, on the other hand, is restricted by definition: being a part of the represented world, he cannot know everything about it.

Uspensky gives an interesting example from Dostoevsky's The Idiot (1868), where the same event is first seen through the eyes of Prince

Myshkin who knows and suspects nothing, and then – two paragraphs later – through those of the external focalizer:

> Rogozhin's eyes glittered and a frenzied smile contorted his face. He raised his right hand and something gleamed in it. The prince did not think of checking it.
>
> (Quoted by Uspensky 1973, p. 82)

The object in Rogozhin's hand is an unspecified 'something' to the unknowing prince. To the narrator-focalizer, on the other hand, it is clearly a knife:

> It must be supposed that some such feeling of sudden horror, together with the other terrible sensations of the moment, had suddenly paralysed Rogozhin and so saved the prince from the inevitable blow of the knife which already was coming at him.
>
> (Quoted by Uspensky 1973, p. 82)[11]

The emotive component

In its emotive transformation, the 'external/internal' opposition yields 'objective' (neutral, uninvolved) v. 'subjective' (coloured, involved) focalization. The subjectivity of an internal focalizer can be seen by comparing two occasions on which Emma Bovary looks at her garden at Tostes. The first occurs before the period of her great *ennui* and is therefore neutral in character:

> The garden, longer than wide, ran between two mud walls covered with espaliered apricot trees, to a thorn hedge that separated it from the field. In the middle was a slate sundial on a brick pedestal; four flower-beds with eglantines surrounded symmetrically the more useful vegetable garden. Right at the bottom, under the spruce bushes, a plaster priest was reading his breviary.
>
> (1965, p. 23. Orig. publ. in French 1857)

The same garden is later seen by Emma as a place of disease, ruin and death, a correlative of her desperate mood at that time:

> On fine days she went down into the garden. The dew had left a silver lace on the cabbages with long transparent threads spreading from one to the other. No birds were to be heard; everything seemed asleep, the fruit tree covered with straw, and the vine, like a great sick serpent under the coping of the wall, along which, on drawing near, one saw the many-footed woodlice crawling. Under the spruce by the hedge-row, the curé in the three-cornered hat reading his breviary had lost his right foot, and the very plaster, scaling off with the frost, had left white scabs on his face.
>
> (1965, p. 46)

Since the garden itself is inanimate, the psychological facet of focalization is relevant only to the human focalizer perceiving it. But when the focalized is also human, his own subjectivity is no less relevant than that of the focalizer. As was said above (pp. 74–5), the focalized can be perceived either from without or from within. The first type restricts all observation to external manifestations, leaving the emotions to be inferred from them, as in Hemingway's 'The Killers' (1928) where the nervousness of the killers is implied by their frequent glances at the clock and their recurrent irritated questions. The second type reveals the 'inner life' of the focalized, either by making him his own focalizer (interior monologues are the best example) or by granting an external focalizer (a narrator-focalizer) the privilege of penetrating the consciousness of the focalized (as in most nineteenth-century novels). When the focalized is seen from within, especially by an external focalizer, indicators such as 'he thought', 'he felt', 'it seemed to him', 'he knew', 'he recognized' often appear in the text. On the other hand, when the inner states of the focalized are left to be implied by external behaviour, modal expressions – suggesting the speculative status of such implication – often occur: 'apparently', 'evidently', 'as if', 'it seemed', etc. Uspensky calls these 'words of estrangement' (1973, p. 85).

The ideological facet

This facet, often referred to as 'the norms of the text', consists of 'a general system of viewing the world conceptually', in accordance with which the events and characters of the story are evaluated (Uspensky 1973, p. 8). In the simplest case, the 'norms' are presented through a single dominant perspective, that of the narrator-focalizer. If additional ideologies emerge in such texts, they become subordinate to the dominant focalizer, thus transforming the other evaluating subjects into objects of evaluation (Uspensky 1973, pp. 8–9). Put differently, the ideology of the narrator-focalizer is usually taken as authoritative, and all other ideologies in the text are evaluated from this 'higher' position. In more complex cases, the single authoritative external focalizer gives way to a plurality of ideological positions whose validity is doubtful in principle. Some of these positions may concur in part or in whole, others may be mutually opposed, the interplay among them provoking a non-unitary, 'polyphonic' reading of the text (Bakhtin 1973. Orig. publ. in Russian 1929). Dostoevsky, of course, immediately comes to mind. In *Crime and Punishment* (1866), for example, the ideology of the text (or its questioning of ideology) emerges from a juxtaposition of Raskolnikov's views with his own performance, as well as with the opinions of Razumihin, Sonia, Svidrigailov, and the anonymous officer in the bar.

A character may represent an ideological position through his way of seeing the world or his behaviour in it, but also – like Raskolnikov – through explicit discussion of his ideology. Similarly, the norms of a narrator-focalizer may be implicit in the orientation he gives to the story, but they can also be formulated explicitly. Thus, in addition to its contribution to focalization, ideology also plays a part in the story (characters), on the one hand, and in narration, on the other. That this may be true of all facets of focalization will be suggested in the concluding paragraph of this chapter.

The interrelations among the various facets

The perceptual, psychological and ideological facets may concur but they may also belong to different, even clashing, focalizers. Thus, in *Great Expectations*, the perceptual focalizer is usually the young, experiencing Pip, whereas the ideology tends to be focalized by the older, narrating Pip (Chatman 1978, p. 158). A similar discrepancy between the psychological and the ideological facets can be found in

Dostoevsky's *The Brothers Karamazov* (1880): the psychology of Fyodor Pavlovich Karamazov is often revealed from within, although he is presented as an unsympathetic character from the ideological point of view (Uspensky 1973, p. 105).

VERBAL INDICATORS OF FOCALIZATION

To say that focalization is conveyed by various verbal indicators is not to cancel the distinction between focalization and narration with which I began. In itself, focalization is non-verbal; however, like everything else in the text, it is expressed by language. The overall language of a text is that of the narrator, but focalization can 'colour' it in a way which makes it appear as a transposition of the perceptions of a separate agent. Thus both the presence of a focalizer other than the narrator and the shift from one focalizer to another may be signalled by language.

An interesting example of such signalling is naming. As Uspensky shows (1973, pp. 20–43), the use of the various names of Napoleon in Tolstoy's *War and Peace* betrays differences as well as changes of attitude toward him. In the early stages, the Russians call him 'Bonaparte', emphasizing his nationality, or even 'Buonaparte', doubling his foreignness by stressing that he is not even French. The French, on the other hand, call him 'Napoleon' and later 'L'empereur Napoleon'. With the progress of his conquests, most Russians switch to 'Napoleon' and those who do not, thereby make a strong national point. Shifts in naming can indicate a change of focalizer within the same paragraph or sentence. Here is an example from the encounter between Napoleon and Prince Andrey who lies wounded on the field of Austerlitz:

> He [Andrey] did not turn his head and did not see the men who, judging from the voices and the thud of hoofs, had ridden up to him and stopped.
>
> They were Napoleon and two adjutants escorting him. Bonaparte, making a tour of the field of battle ... was inspecting the dead and wounded. ...
>
> (1971, p. 310. Orig. publ. in Russian 1864–9)

As Uspensky says, 'We may suspect a transition from the point of view of a detached observer (who uses the name 'Napoleon') to the point of view of Prince Andrey (who would use the name 'Bonaparte' because it corresponds to his changed attitude toward Napoleon at this moment of the narrative)' (1973, p. 31).[12]

But names are not the only verbal means of indicating focalization. The whole gamut of stylistic possibilities has not yet been established, nor is it specific to narrative. I shall therefore limit myself to a few examples from Joyce's 'Araby' (1961. Orig. publ. 1914).[13] In this narrative, an adult narrator tells about himself as a child (of an unspecified age). His language is sometimes 'coloured' by his perceptions at the time of narration (external focalization), sometimes by those of his younger self (internal focalization), and sometimes remains ambiguous between the two. A sentence like 'I had never spoken to her, except for a few casual words, and yet her name was like a summons to all my foolish blood' (p. 28) betrays the adult narrator as focalizer through the evaluative adjective 'foolish'. Similarly, although the lexis and syntax of 'I forgot whether I answered yes or no' (p. 29) could easily be attributed to a child by virtue of its simplicity, forgetting can only be recognized in retrospect. The words 'I forgot' thus point to an external focalizer by signalling temporal and cognitive distance from the event. On the other hand, the comparison of the silence of the deserted bazaar to that of a church – 'I recognized a silence like that which pervades a church after a service' (p. 32) – reflects the child's association between the world of religion within which he was brought up with the world of the bazaar which he endowed with a quasi-religious dimension. For the child, the disappointment is similar when both rituals are over. Another indicator of an internal child-focalizer is the emotive, non-sequitur sounding formulation of the causal explanation in the following passage:

> I found a few paper-covered books, the pages of which were curled and damp: *The Abbot* by Walter Scott, *The Devout Communicant*, and *The Memoirs of Vidocq*. I liked the last best because its leaves were yellow.

> (p. 27)

Perhaps most interesting are those cases where choice between an external and an internal focalizer is problematic or impossible. Take, for example, 'I imagined that I bore my chalice safely through a throng of foes' (p. 29). The language is that of the narrator, but the focalizer can be either the narrator or the child. As the vision of the child, the stress is on the world of religious ceremonies in which the child imagines himself a hero. As the vision of the narrator, the stress is on the cliché nature of the child's imagination, and the tone is ironic. Or consider the last sentence: 'Gazing up into darkness I saw myself as a creature driven and derided by vanity; and my eyes burned with anguish and anger' (p. 33). The alliteration in 'driven and derided', 'anguish and anger' is obviously that of the narrator, as is the choice of 'gazing' which echoes the description of the houses in the opening paragraph ('gazed at one another') and the link established between the 'blindness' of the child and the 'blind street' of the beginning. But is the self-awareness ('I saw myself') that of the child in the time of the experience or that of the adult years later? The sentence offers no definitive clue.

In this chapter, focalization was treated as a textual factor relating to both story and narration. This view can be challenged by the suggestion that focalization is not only related to these aspects of narrative but actually subsumed within them, thus disappearing from the analysis of 'text' altogether (Ron, unpublished). If the focalizer is a character, the argument goes, then his acts of perception are part of the story. If he is the narrator, focalization is just one of many rhetorical strategies at his disposal. This hypothesis is not yet developed enough to carry full conviction, but in the future it may modify the post-Genettian theory presented here.

7

NARRATION: LEVELS AND VOICES

THE PARTICIPANTS IN THE NARRATIVE COMMUNICATION SITUATION

Seeking to articulate the views of narration promulgated most notably by Booth (1961) within a semiotic model of communication, Chatman (1978, p. 151) comes up with the following diagram:

| Real author | ··➤ | Implied author | ➤ | (Narrator) | ➤ | (Narratee) | ➤ | Implied reader | ··➤ | Real reader |

Of the six participants enumerated in this diagram two are left outside the narrative transaction proper: the real author and his equally real counterpart, the real reader. In the text, they are 'represented' by substitute agents which Booth and numerous others (e.g. Iser 1974; Perry 1979) call the 'implied author' and 'implied reader'.[1] More than just a textual stance, Booth's implied author appears to be an anthropomorphic entity, often designated as 'the author's second self' (1961, p. 67 and elsewhere). According to this view, the implied author is the governing consciousness of the work as a whole, the source of the norms embodied in the work. Its relation to the real author is admitted to be of great psychological complexity, and has barely been analysed, except to suggest (Booth 1961, p. 75) that implied authors are often far superior in intelligence and moral standards to the actual men and women who are real authors. In any event, it has been put forward that the two need not be, and in fact are often not, identical. An author may embody in a work ideas, beliefs, emotions other than or even quite opposed to those he has in real life; he may also embody different ideas, beliefs and emotions in different works. Thus while the flesh-and-blood author is subject to the vicissitudes of real life, the implied author of a particular work is conceived as a stable entity, ideally consistent with itself within the work.

Distinct from the real author, the implied author also differs from the narrator. Most readers intuitively feel that the implied authors of Browning's 'My Last Duchess' (1842) or Bierce's 'Oil of Dog' (1909–12) for example do not subscribe to the norms of the narrators of these texts. In presenting the distinction between implied author and narrator, Chatman seems to give it a specifically semiotic interpretation:

> Unlike the narrator, the implied author can *tell* us nothing. He, or better, *it* has no voice, no direct means of communicating. It instructs us silently, through the design of the whole, with all the voices, by all the means it has chosen to let us learn.
>
> (1978, p. 148)

Thus, while the narrator can only be defined circularly as the narrative voice' or 'speaker' of a text, the implied author is – in opposition and by definition – voiceless and silent. In this sense the implied author must be seen as a construct inferred and assembled by the reader from all the components of the text. Indeed, speaking of the implied author as a construct based on the text seems to me far safer than imagining it as a personified consciousness or 'second self'.

Like the implied author, the implied reader is also a construct, and just as the former differs from both real author and narrator, so the latter is distinct from both real reader and narratee (see pp. 118–19).

According to Chatman, every text has an implied author and implied reader, but a narrator and a narratee are optional (hence put in parenthesis in his diagram) (p. 150). When the latter are present, the communication proceeds from implied author to narrator to narratee and finally to the implied reader. When a narrator and a narratee are absent, communication is confined to the implied author and the implied reader.

This last point is one of two major difficulties I find in Chatman's scheme. If the implied author is only a construct, if its defining property (as opposed to the narrator) is that it 'has no voice, no direct means of communicating' (p. 148), then it seems a contradiction in terms to cast it in the role of the addresser in a communication situation.[2] This is not to deny the significance of the concept of implied author or its usefulness in the analysis or even mere comprehension of narrative fiction. On the contrary, I believe that this concept is important and often crucial in determining the reader's attitude to such a major component as the narrator (mostly in cases of unreliability; see pp. 100–3). My claim is that if it is to be consistently distinguished from the real author and the narrator, the notion of the implied author must be de-personified, and is best considered as a set of implicit norms rather than as a speaker or a voice (i.e. a subject). It follows, therefore, that the implied author cannot literally be a participant in the narrative communication situation.[3]

My second objection to Chatman's scheme concerns his treatment of the narrator and the narratee. Whereas the first modification I propose is the exclusion of the implied author and reader from a description of the communication situation, my second suggestion calls for the inclusion of the narrator and the narratee as constitutive, not just optional, factors in narrative communication. Thus I cannot accept the statement that 'just as there may or may not be a narrator, there may or may not be a narratee' (Chatman 1978, p.150).[4] In my view there is always a teller in the tale, at least in the sense that any utterance or record of an utterance presupposes someone who has uttered it.[5] Even when a narrative text presents passages of pure dialogue, manuscript found in a bottle, or forgotten letters and diaries, there is in addition to the speakers or writers of this discourse a 'higher' narratorial authority responsible for 'quoting' the dialogue or 'transcribing' the written records.

Unlike Chatman, I define the narrator minimally, as the agent which at the very least narrates or engages in some activity serving the needs of narration. The writing of a diary or a letter is thus a form of narration, although the one who writes it may not intend to or be conscious of narrating. Chatman, on the other hand, believes that 'Though diary-entries may and often do narrate, they need not. (A story may be cast in epistolary form in which every sentence expresses only the then-and-there relationship between the correspondents' (1978, p. 170). Instead of Chatman's dichotomy between absent and present narrators, I propose to distinguish forms and degrees of perceptibility of the narrator in the text.

The same goes for the narratee. For me, the narratee is the agent which is at the very least implicitly addressed by the narrator. (A narratee of this kind is always implied, even when the narrator becomes his own narratee. This is the case of Camus's *L'Etranger* (1942) which Chatman, unlike myself, considers a narrative without a narratee.

Only four of Chatman's six participants are thus relevant to my conception of narration: the real author, the real reader, the narrator, the narratee. Furthermore, as I have suggested in the introduction, the empirical process of communication between author and reader is less relevant to the poetics of narrative fiction than its counterpart in the text. This chapter will therefore deal with two participants only: the fictional narrator and the fictional narratee. The implied author and reader will be mentioned when relevant, but a fuller analysis of these constructs will be reserved for chapter 9.

THE RELATIONS BETWEEN NARRATION AND STORY

Temporal relations

Since narration is an event like any other, it can entertain various temporal relations with the events of the story. These are classified by Genette under four headings (1972, pp. 228–34). Common sense tells us that events may be narrated only after they happen ('ulterior narration'), as in Fielding's *Tom Jones* (1749), Dickens's *Great Expectations* (1860/61) and Woolf's *Mrs Dalloway* (1925), to mention only a few texts where this most frequent form of narration is used. The distance between the narration and the events varies from text to text: around fifteen years in *Great Expectations*, one day in *L'Etranger*. But a narration after the event (normally in the past tense) is not the only possibility. Much less frequent, for obvious reasons, is a narration which precedes the events ('anterior narration'). It is a kind of predictive narration, generally using the future tense, but sometimes the present. Whereas examples abound in Biblical prophecies, complete modern texts written in the predictive vein are rare. Instead, this type of narration tends to appear in narratives within narratives in the form of prophecies, curses or dreams of fictional characters. Such is the vision cum explanation of the future given to Adam by the Angel Michael in Books XI–XII of Milton's *Paradise Lost* (1667), a narrative whose predictive nature is confirmed by the historical knowledge of the modern reader. Any prolepsis is, of course, a 'pocket' of anterior narration.

A third type of narration is simultaneous with the action, e.g. reporting or diary entries.[6] In Butor's *La Modification* the narrator, addressing himself in the second person, seems to be verbalizing his actions while performing them:

> You have put your left foot on the copper rabbet, and with your right shoulder you are trying in vain to push the sliding panel a little further ... then, your suitcase ... you are lifting it up and you feel your muscles and tendons.
>
> (1957, p. 9. My translation)

When telling and acting are not simultaneous but follow each other in alternation, narration is of the fourth type, namely 'intercalated'. Classic examples of this type are epistolary novels, such as Laclos's *Les liaisons dangereuses* (1782), in which the writing of letters often serves both to narrate an event of the recent past and to trigger an event of the near future.

The distance between story and narration is not the only temporal determination of the latter. In principle, narration also has a duration (i.e. the time it takes to tell something). And yet most fiction conventionally ignores this duration and treats narration as if it were instantaneous (narratives within narratives are often an exception to the rule). The paradoxical result of ignoring this convention is wittily dramatized in Sterne's *Tristram Shandy* (1760). After a whole year of writing, Tristram realizes that all he has recorded is the first day of his life. Narration thus always lags behind living, and consequently the more he writes, the more he will have to write about. To complete the enterprise of writing thus seems impossible.

Like the duration of the act of narration, the place in which it occurs need not be mentioned, nor does the reader feel the need for such specification. Narratives within narratives are again an exception. Conrad's *Heart of Darkness* (1902), for example, describes in detail the ship on which Marlow's narration takes place. It also establishes many analogies between Marlow's narration and the story he narrates: both narration and events happen in the heart of darkness, in both cases a character (Marlow, Kurtz) is reduced to a voice, etc.

Subordination relations: narrative levels

Most of what was said up to now was concerned with the narration of the story. But there may also be narration in the story. (A character whose actions are the object of narration can himself in turn engage in narrating a story. Within his story there may, of course, be yet another character who narrates another story, and so on in infinite regress. Such narratives within narratives create a stratification of levels whereby each inner narrative is subordinate to the narrative within which it is embedded.

In this hierarchical structure, the highest level is the one immediately superior to the first narrative and concerned with its narration (Genette 1972 calls this the 'extradiegetic level', his 'diegesis' being roughly analogous to my 'story'). It is at this level that the narrator of Chaucer's *The Canterbury Tales* (1390–1400 approx.) presents the pilgrims, the adult Pip of *Great Expectations* tells about his childhood, and Portonoy addresses his ' complaint' to the silent psychiatrist. Immediately subordinate to the extradiegetic level is the diegetic level narrated by it, that is the events themselves: the pilgrims' journey to the shrine of St Thomas à Becket, Pip's falling in love with Estella, Portonoy's struggles with his Jewish mother. The events may include speech-acts of narration – whether oral, as when Chaucer's pilgrims take turns at telling stories, or written, like Sebastian's novels in Nabokov's *The Real*

Life of Sebastian Knight (1941). The stories told by fictional characters, e.g. the exploits of the pardoner, constitute a second degree narrative, hence a hypodiegetic level (i.e. a level 'below' another level of diegesis)[7]. Narration is always at a higher narrative level than the story it narrates. Thus the diegetic level is narrated by an extradiegetic narrator, the hypodiegetic level by a diegetoic (intradiegetic) one.

Hypodiegetic narratives may have various functions in relation to the narratives within which they are embedded. These functions are sometimes present separately, sometimes in combination, thus:

1 *Actional function:* some hypodiegetic narratives maintain or advance the action of the first narrative by the sheer fact of being narrated, regardless (or almost regardless) of their content. *A Thousand and One Nights* is a classical example. Scheherezade's life depends on her narration, and the only condition her stories have to fulfil is to sustain the Sultan's attention.

2 *Explicative function:* the hypodiegetic level offers an explanation of the diegetic level, answering some such question as 'What were the events leading to the present situation?' In this case, it is the story narrated and not the act of narration itself that is of primary importance. In Faulkner's *Absalom, Absalom!* (1936), Thomas Sutpen's narration of his childhood to General Compson, especially of the insulting confrontation with the negro servant (a hypo-hypodiegetic level), explains how Sutpen lost his innocence and came to be the self-reliant, a-moral person he is.

3 *Thematic function:* the relations established between the hypodiegetic and the diegetic levels are those of analogy, i.e. similarity and contrast. This function predominates in Nabokov's *The Real Life of Sebastian Knight*. To give one example out of many: the story of Sebastian's last novel, *The Doubtful Asphodel* (hypo-hypodiegetic level) is strikingly analogous to V's quest for 'the real life' of his half-brother, Sebastian (diegetic level). The subject of Sebastian's novel is a dying man who has a secret, an absolute truth, to divulge and who dies before uttering the word which could have changed the lives of all those who could have benefited from the disclosure. In a similar fashion, V desperately tries to reach the dying Sebastian in the belief that 'He has something to tell me, something of boundless importance' (1971, p. 162. Orig. publ. 1941), but Sebastian dies, and it is too late for the extraordinary

revelation to come from his lips (on this and other analogies in this novel, see Rimmon 1976b, pp. 489–512).

An analogy which verges on identity, making the hypodiegetic level a mirror and reduplication of the diegetic, is known in French as *mise en abyme*. It can be described as the equivalent in narrative fiction of something like Matisse's famous painting of a room in which a miniature version of the same paintings hangs on one of the walls. Ever since Gide's expression of a predilection for *mise en abyme*, described in his journals as a transposition of the theme of a work to the level of the characters (1948, p. 41), the technique has been much discussed, in particular in the French-speaking world (e.g. Ricardou 1967, 1971; Dällenbach 1977; Bal 1978). A famous example from Gide's own work is *The Counterfeiters* (1949) where a character is engaged in writing a novel similar to the novel in which he appears. Unfortunately, because of the limited scope of the present study, I can only mention *mise en abyme* briefly, without going into the variety of its types, functions and significance.

The transition from one narrative level to another is in principle effected by the act of narration which draws the reader's attention to the shift. Thus in *The Canterbury Tales*:

> And he began to speak, with right good cheer,
> His tale anon, as it is written here.
> *The General Prologue*, ll. 857–8

Sometimes, however, the transition is not marked, and the discreteness of levels is transgressed. When the narrator in Melville's *Pierre, or the Ambiguities* addresses the reader with a comment like 'While Pierre and Lucy are now rolling along under the elms, let it be said who Lucy Tartan was' (1964, p. 45. Orig. publ. 1852), he treats the narration (extradiegetic level) as if it were contemporary with the narrated events (diegetic level) and should therefore fill-in 'dead periods' in the story. The narrator's digressions in *Tristram Shandy* have a similar effect, as when the presentation of Mrs Shandy is interrupted by: 'In this attitude I am determined to let her stand for five minutes: till I bring up the affairs of the kitchen ... to the same period' (1967, p. 353). In addition to undermining the separation between narration and story,

Tristram Shandy also places narratee and story on the same level: it does so when asking the 'dear reader' to help Tristram reach his bed (1967, p. 285).

Modern self-conscious texts often play with narrative levels in order to question the borderline between reality and fiction or to suggest that there may be no reality apart from its narration. Christine Brooke-Rose's *Thru* (1975) is an extreme example of the interchangeability of narrative levels.[8] The novel repeatedly reverses the hierarchy, transforming a narrated object into a narrating agent and vice versa. The very distinction between outside and inside, container and contained, narrating subject and narrated object, higher and lower level collapses, resulting in a paradox which the text itself puts in a nutshell: 'Whoever you invented invented you too' (1975, p. 53).

A TYPOLOGY OF NARRATORS

The narrative level to which the narrator belongs, the extent of his participation in the story, the degree of perceptibility of his role, and finally his reliability are crucial factors in the reader's understanding of and attitude to the story. It is therefore according to these criteria that the variety of narrators will be presented. The criteria are not mutually exclusive and allow for cross-combinations between the different types.

Narrative level

A narrator who is, as it were, 'above' or superior to the story he narrates is 'extradiegetic', like the level of which he is a part (Genette 1972, pp. 255–6). To this category belong the narrators of Fielding's *Tom Jones* (1749), Balzac's *Père Goriot* (1834), Lawrence's *Sons and Lovers* (1913), but also – as I shall soon argue – that of Dickens's *Great Expectations* (1860/61). On the other hand, if the narrator is also a diegetic character in the first narrative told by the extradiegetic narrator, then he is a second-degree, or intradiegetic narrator (Genette 1972, pp. 255–6). Examples are Marlow in Conrad's *Heart of Darkness* and the pardoner in *The Canterbury Tales*. There can also be narrators of a third degree (i.e. hypodiegetic), fourth degree (hypo-hypodiegetic), etc. In James's *The*

Turn of the Screw (1898) the extradiegetic narrator is the anonymous 'I', the intradiegetic one is Douglas, and the hypodiegetic narrator is the governess.

Extent of participation in the story

Both extradiegetic and intradiegetic narrators can be either absent from or present in the story they narrate. (A narrator who does not participate in the story is called 'heterodiegetic' (Genette 1972, pp. 255–6), whereas the one who takes part in it, at least in some manifestation of his 'self', is 'homodiegetic' (pp. 255–6).

The extradiegetic narrators of Tom Jones, Père Goriot, and Sons and Lovers are in no sense participants in the stories they narrate (hence they are both extradiegetic and heterodiegetic). It is precisely their being absent from the story and their higher narratorial authority in relation to it that confers on such narrators the quality which has often been called 'omniscience'. 'Omniscience' is perhaps an exaggerated term, especially for modern extradiegetic narrators. Nevertheless, the characteristics connoted by it are still relevant, namely: familiarity, in principle, with the characters' innermost thoughts and feelings; knowledge of past, present and future; presence in locations where characters are supposed to be unaccompanied (e.g. on a lonely stroll or during a love-scene in a locked room); and knowledge of what happens in several places at the same time (Ewen 1974, pp. 144–6).

Compare Fielding's, Balzac's and Lawrence's narrators to Pip of Great Expectations. Like them, the adult Pip is a higher narratorial authority in relation to the story which he narrates, as it were, from 'above'. Although not omniscient in principle, when narrating the story he knows 'everything' about it, like the former extradiegetic narrators. He knows the solution to the enigma concerning the identity of the mysterious benefactor (a crucial detail he withholds from the reader for a long time); he has knowledge of simultaneous events happening in different places, e.g. Estella's marriage and divorce during the period her childhood-admirer spends in London and Cairo; he is aware of the characters' innermost emotions, e.g. the need for revenge motivating Miss Havisham's manipulation of Estella to break men's hearts, etc. However, unlike the other extradiegetic narrators, Pip tells a story in which a younger version of himself participated. He is thus a homo- not a heterodiegetic narrator.

Like extradiegetic narrators, intradiegetic ones can also be either heterodiegetic or homodiegetic. Scheherezade is a fictional character in a story narrated by an extradiegetic narrator. However, in the stories she herself narrates, she does not appear as a character. She is therefore an intradiegetic-heterodiegetic narrator. On the other hand, Chaucer's pardoner and Lockwood in *Wuthering Heights* (1847) narrate stories in which they also participate as characters: they are therefore intradiegetic-homodiegetic.

The degree of participation of homodiegetic narrators (be they extradiegetic or intradiegetic) varies from case to case. Pip (extra-homodiegetic) and the pardoner (intra-homodiegetic) play a central role in the respective stories they narrate (protagonists-narrators) – or, put differently, they narrate their own story (auto-diegetic narrators, in Genette's terms). On the other hand, Lockwood's role is subsidiary (witness-narrator).

Degree of perceptibility

This ranges from the maximum of covertness (often mistaken for a complete absence of a narrator) to the maximum of overtness.[9] Hemingway's 'The Killers', almost entirely restricted to dialogue, is often praised by critics for the covertness of its narrator (see example in chapter 4, p. 54). Nevertheless, the dialogue is 'quoted' by someone, the same 'someone' who identifies the speakers ('Nick asked', 'Al said', etc.) and describes the restaurant as well as the characters' external appearance. Who could that 'someone' be if not a narrator? Moreover, at three points in the text the narrator's presence becomes more perceptible, betraying knowledge of the past: 'Henry's had been made over from a saloon into a lunch-counter' (1965, p. 61. Orig. publ. 1928), Nick 'had never had a towel in his mouth before' (p. 65), Ole Anderson 'had been a heavyweight prize-fighter' (p. 66). Thus a few signs of overtness can be detected even in a text whose narrator is almost purely covert. In less pure cases, there are many signs of overtness which Chatman (1978, pp. 220–52) lists in mounting order of perceptibility:

1 *Description of setting:* This relatively minimal sign of a narrator's presence occurs even in Hemingway. Consider, for example, the opening of 'Hills like White Elephants':

> The hills across the valley of the Ebro were long and white. On this side there was no shade and no trees and the station was between two lines of rails in the sun. Close against the side of the station there was the warm shadow of the building and a curtain, made of strings of bamboo beads, hung across the open door into the bar, to keep out the flies.
>
> (1965, p. 51. Orig. publ. 1928)[10]

In a play or a film, all this would be shown directly. In narrative fiction, it has to be said in language, and the language is that of a narrator.

2 *Identification of characters:* Statements like 'Emma Woodhouse, handsome, clever, and rich, with a comfortable home and happy disposition . . .' (Austen 1974, p. 37. Orig. publ. 1816) or 'Mrs Dalloway said she would buy the flowers herself' (Woolf 1974, p. 5. Orig. publ. 1925) show prior 'knowledge' of the character on the part of the narrator who can therefore identify the former to the reader at the very beginning of the text. Such statements also imply an assumption that the narratee-reader does not share this knowledge, an assumption which characterizes one of the narrator's roles, i.e. to communicate to others what they don't know. Austen's narrator goes beyond identification to provide a whole characterization of the heroine. Woolf's narrator, on the other hand 'merely identifies, relegating additional details to bracketed statements either in the form of observations by other characters or in that of Mrs Dalloway's own thoughts. Here is a neighbour's observation from which we learn about Clarissa's age and illness: 'a touch of the bird about her, of the jay, blue-green, light, vivacious, though she was over fifty, and grown very white since her illness' (1974, p. 6). Although the narrator's presence is much less perceptible in *Mrs Dalloway* than it is in *Emma*, it is felt even in the former through the identification.

3 *Temporal summary:* 'Summary presupposes a desire to account for time-passage, to satisfy questions in a narratee's mind about what has

happened in the interval. An account cannot but draw attention to the one who felt obliged to make such an account' (Chatman 1978, p. 223). The brief summary of Albino's whole life in the opening of Nabokov's *Laughter in the Dark* as well as the compression of sixteen years in Flaubert's *Sentimental Education* (to mention only examples of summary quoted in an earlier chapter, pp. 53–5) imply the presence of a narrator as well as his notion of what should be told in detail and what could be narrated with greater conciseness.

4 *Definition of character:* Whereas an identification of a character implies only the narrator's prior knowledge about or acquaintance with him, definition also suggests an abstraction, generalization or summing up on the part of the narrator as well as a desire to present such labelling as authoritative characterization. This is how Henry James's narrator defines the heroine of *The Portrait of a Lady:*

> Isabel Archer was a young person of many theories; her imagination was remarkably active. . . . Her thoughts were a tangle of vague outlines which had never been corrected by the judgement of people speaking with authority. In matters of opinion she had had her own way, and it had led her into a thousand ridiculous zigzags.
>
> (1964, p. 49. Orig. publ. 1881)

Such definitions tend to carry more weight when given by an extradiegetic narrator than by an intradiegetic one.

5 *Reports of what characters did not think or say:* A narrator who can tell things of which the characters are either unconscious or which they deliberately conceal is clearly felt as an independent source of information. An example from Hardy's *Tess of the D'Urbervilles:*

> Every day, every hour, brought to him one more little stroke of her nature, and to her one more of his. Tess was trying to lead a repressed life, but she little divined the strength of her own vitality.
>
> (1963, p. 148. Orig. publ. 1891)

6 *Commentary:* Commentary can be either on the story or on the narration. One form of commentary on the story is *interpretation,* as when the narrator of Carson McCullers's 'The Sojourner' explains the

state of mind behind the ageing character's sudden tenderness toward his mistress's son, for whom he has always had neither time nor patience: 'With inner desperation he pressed the child close – as though an emotion as protean as his love could dominate the pulse of time' (1971, p. 346. Orig. publ. 1951). Interpretations often provide information not only about their direct object but also about the interpreter. The narrator of James's *The Sacred Fount* (1901), for example, develops a whole theory about the possibility of vampire-like relations among four of the guests in the country-house he visits. From his elaborate speculations we learn at least as much about him (his highly developed imagination, his priggishness, his tendency to polarize human beings, etc.) as we do about the characters whose behaviour he interprets.

Perhaps more revealing of the narrator's moral stand are *judgements*. Like many interpretations and definitions, the passage quoted above from *The Portrait of a Lady* verges on judgement. But there are other passages in the same novel which are more directly judgemental:

> It may be affirmed without delay that Isabel was probably very liable to the sin of self-esteem; she often surveyed with complacency the field of her own nature; she was in the habit of taking for granted, on scanty evidence, that she was right; she treated herself to occasions of homage.
>
> (p. 50)

The third type of commentary, *generalization*, is not restricted to a specific character, event, or situation but extends the significance of the particular case in a way which purportedly applies to a group, a society or humanity at large. Such is the beginning of Tolstoy's *Anna Karenina*: 'Happy families are all alike; every unhappy family is unhappy in its own way' (1950, p. 3. Orig. publ. in Russian 1873–6).

Unlike interpretation, judgement and generalization relating to the story, commentary on the narration is concerned not with the represented world but with the problems of representing it. In Dickens's *Bleak House*, Esther opens her narrative thus: 'I have a great deal of difficulty in beginning to write my portion of these pages, for I know I am not clever. I always knew that' (1964, p. 30. Orig. publ. 1853).

Esther apologetically comments on her feeling of inadequacy as a narrator, but her reservations do not undermine the fictional reality of the story she narrates. Compare this with Beckett's *Watt* where the history of the Lynch family is followed by a footnote:

> Five generations, twenty-eight souls, nine hundred and eight years, such was the proud record of the Lynch family when Watt entered Mr Knott's service."
>
> 'The figures given here are incorrect. The consequent calculations are therefore doubly erroneous.
>
> (1972, p. 101. Orig. publ. in French 1953)

The very use of a footnote in a work of fiction is unusual and automatically draws attention to the presence of a narrator reflecting on his own narration. Moreover, the footnote contradicts the information given in the text, thus undermining either the credibility of the text or the reliability of the narrator or both. In any case, it emphasizes the status of the text as artifice, provoking reflections about fictionality and textuality which are typical of self-conscious narratives.

Reliability

A reliable narrator is one whose rendering of the story and commentary on it the reader is supposed to take as an authoritative account of the fictional truth. An unreliable narrator, on the other hand, is one whose rendering of the story and/or commentary on it the reader has reasons to suspect. There can, of course, be different degrees of unreliability. But how can the reader know whether he is supposed to trust or distrust the narrator's account? What indications does the text give him one way or the other? Signs of unreliability are perhaps easier to specify, and reliability can then be negatively defined by their absence.

The main sources of unreliability are the narrator's limited knowledge, his personal involvement, and his problematic value-scheme. A young narrator would be a clear case of limited knowledge (and understanding), e.g. the adolescent who tells the disturbing events of his recent past in Salinger's *The Catcher in the Rye* (1951). An idiot-narrator would be another, like Faulkner's Benjy in the first section of *The Sound and the Fury* (1931). However, adult and mentally normal narrators also quite often tell things they do not fully know. Thus Rosa in *Absalom, Absalom!* narrates in great detail Sutpen's fight with his negroes in the presence of his children, and then adds: 'But I was not there. I was not there to see the two Sutpen faces . . . looking down through the square entrance to the loft' (1972, p. 30).

Rosa's narration is suspect not only because of her limited knowledge but also because of her personal involvement, her hatred of Sutpen, her undying sense of injury resulting from his insulting proposal that he would marry her only if they succeed in having a male child first. Consequently, she presents him as a demon, a characterization clearly distorted by her subjective (even if justified) rage. What is suspect in this instance is Rosa's evaluation of Sutpen's acts rather than her reporting of the events themselves (as in the previous example).

The third potential source of unreliability is the colouring of the narrator's account by a questionable value-scheme. A narrator's moral values are considered questionable if they do not tally with those of the implied author of the given work. If the implied author does share the narrator's values then the latter is reliable in this respect, no matter how objectionable his views may seem to some readers. The trouble with the foregoing statement, however, is that the values (or 'norms') of the implied author are notoriously difficult to arrive at. Various factors in the text may indicate a gap between the norms of the implied author and those of the narrator: when the facts contradict the narrator's views, the latter is judged to be unreliable (but how does one establish the 'real facts' behind the narrator's back?); when the outcome of the action proves the narrator wrong, a doubt is retrospectively cast over his reliability in reporting earlier events; when the views of other characters consistently clash with the narrator's, suspicion may arise in the reader's mind; and when the narrator's language contains internal contradictions, double-edged images, and the like, it may have a boomerang effect, undermining the reliability of its user.

Let us take as a concrete example a funny and terrifying passage from Ambrose Bierce's 'Oil of Dog':

> My name is Boffer Bings. I was born of honest parents in one of the humbler walks of life, my father being a manufacturer of dog-oil and

my mother having a small studio in the shadow of the village church, where she disposed of unwelcome babes. . . . It had been my custom to throw the babes into the river which nature had thoughtfully provided for the purpose, but that night I did not dare to leave the oilery for fear of the constable. 'After all', I said to myself, 'it cannot greatly matter if I put it into this cauldron. My father will never know the bones from those of a puppy, and the few deaths which may result from administering another kind of oil for the incomparable *ol.can.* are not important in a population which increases so rapidly.

(1952, p. 800. Orig. publ. 1909–12)

Contrasts and incongruities in the narrator's language alert us to a possible unreliability in the narrator's evaluations, though not necessarily in his reporting of facts. How can one speak of a mother who disposes of unwelcome babies (and, moreover, does so in the shadow of the village church) as 'honest'? How can one describe nature as thoughtfully providing a river into which these unfortunate babes can be thrown? Understatements operate in a similar way: having thrown one baby into the cauldron, Boffer is only concerned about making sure that his father would not distinguish the bones of a baby from those of a puppy. And what if some deaths result from this manoeuvre? Well, these 'are not important in a population which increases so rapidly'. The sequel of the action also suggests that the horrors practised by the Bings family cannot be treated lightly. When the intervention of the townspeople forbids the continuation of the business, the father and mother, eager to continue their professions, attempt to take each other's life and end by boiling together in the cauldron: 'A disagreeable instance of domestic infelicity', the narrator comments in his understating tone (p. 803).

Interestingly, even a passage with so many markers of unreliability is problematic. Instead of being considered unreliable, and hence the butt of the irony shared by the implied author and reader, couldn't the narrator be seen as ironically telling the experiences of his younger self? Couldn't the contrasts, incongruities and understatements be the narrator's way of exposing the horror and immorality of which the child was innocent? As a counter-argument one may recall that even after the events the narrator does not feel remorse for the immorality of his youthful behaviour, but only 'for a heedless act [throwing the baby into the dog cauldron] entailing so dismal a commercial disaster' (p. 803). In other words, he deplores a tactical error, not a moral fault, and this is what the implied author invites the reader to criticize. But self-irony may operate here too, implying the horror of all the rest precisely by confining the explicit indignation to the most morally neutral act.

Uncertainty is not confined to cases where both unrealiability and irony could be attributed to the narrator. Many texts make it difficult to decide whether the narrator is reliable or unreliable, and if unreliable – to what extent. Some texts – which may be called ambiguous narratives – make such a decision impossible, putting the reader in a position of constant oscillation between mutually exclusive alternatives. The governess in James's *The Turn of the Screw*, to take the most famous example, can be seen as a reliable narrator telling the story of two haunted children, but she can also be considered an unreliable, neurotic narrator, unwittingly reporting her own hallucinations.

A covert extradiegetic narrator, especially when he is also heterodiegetic, is likely to be reliable. Cases like Robbe-Grillet's *Le Voyeur* (1955), where such a narrator continuously contradicts himself, thereby becoming unreliable, are extremely unusual. However, when an extradiegetic narrator becomes more overt, his chances of being fully reliable are diminished, since his interpretations, judgements, generalizations are not always compatible with the norms of the implied author. Intradiegetic narrators, especially when they are also homodiegetic, are on the whole more fallible than extradiegetic ones, because are also characters in the fictional world. As such, they are subject to limited knowledge, personal involvement, and problematic value-schemes, often giving rise to the possibility of unreliability.[11]

NARRATEES

Although only scanty attention was paid to narratees before the last decade, they are as indispensable to narrative fiction as narrators (important recent studies of the narratee, on which my account is based, are Prince 1973, pp. 178–96; Genette 1972, pp. 265–7; Chatman 1978, pp. 253–61). The narratee is sometimes fully personified, sometimes not. In any case, the narratee is the agent addressed by the narrator, and all the criteria for classifying the latter also apply to the former.

Using narrative level as a criterion, we can distinguish between a narratee who is 'above' the first narrative, i.e. extradiegetic, and one who is also a character within the first narrative, i.e. intradiegetic. Extradiegetic narratees can be addressed directly by some narrator, e.g. the Sultan in *A Thousand and One Nights* as, say, in *Mrs Dalloway*. Intradiegetic narratees are always addressed directly by some narrator, e.g. the Sultan in *A Thousand and One Nights* being addressed by Scheherezade, or Marlow's shipmates aboard the *Nellie* listening to the latter's story in *Heart of Darkness*. The narratee is, by definition, situated at the same narrative level as the narrator (Genette 1972, p. 265). The same narrative may, of course, contain both an extradiegetic and an intradiegetic narratee, just as it may include both types of narrators.

Taking the second criterion, i.e. participation in the story, we can distinguish between those narratees who play a part in the events narrated to them (e.g. Mme de Merteuil, Valmont, or Cécile in *Les liaisons dangereuses*) and those who do not (e.g. the psychiatrist in *Portnoy's Complaint*).

Like narrators, narratees can be either covert or overt. A covert narratee is no more than the silent addressee of the narrator, whereas an overt one can be made perceptible through the narrator's inferences of his possible answers (Camus, *La Chute*, 1956), the narratee's actual answers or comments (the pilgrims in *The Canterbury Tales*), or his actions (*Les liaisons dangereuses*).

As Chatman has shown (1978, p. 260), not only the narrator but the narratee as well can be either reliable or unreliable. The extradiegetic narratee (parallel to or identical with the implied reader) is granted reliability, without which his status as distinct from the real reader would be meaningless. Intradiegetic narratees, on the other hand, can be unreliable, and hence the butt of the irony shared by the implied author and reader. This happens 'when the values of the implied reader evoked by the implied author are at odds with those of the narratee evoked by the narrator' (Chatman 1978, pp. 260–1). Tristram Shandy, gentleman and narrator, enters into a dialogue with a narratee addressed as 'Madam', whose unreliability he repeatedly stresses:

– How could you, Madam, be so inattentive in reading the last chapter? I told you in it, *that my father was not a papist.* – Papist! You told me no such thing, Sir. Madam, I beg leave to repeat it over again, That I told you as plain, at least, as words, by direct inference, could tell you such a thing. – Then, Sir, I must have missed a page. – No, Madam, you have not missed a word. – Then I was asleep, Sir. – My pride, Madam, cannot allow you that refuge.

(1967, p. 82)

'Madam' is thus to be distinguished from the implied reader (or extradiegetic narratee) whose attentive perusal of this novel is thereby indirectly solicited.

The foregoing discussion of the participants in the narrative communication situation, the temporal and hierarchical relations between narration and story, the various kinds of narrators, and the narratee, was concerned with the rendering of both events and speech. Indeed, speech is an event like any other, but it has characteristics specific to it, and these add interesting complexities to the problem of narration. It is to the rendering of speech that the next chapter will be devoted.

8

NARRATION: SPEECH REPRESENTATION

A BRIEF HISTORICAL ACCOUNT: DIEGESIS AND MIMESIS

In the third book of Plato's *Republic* Socrates posits a distinction between two ways of rendering speech: *diegesis* and *mimesis*. The characteristic feature of diegesis is that 'the poet himself is the speaker and does not even attempt to suggest to us that anyone but himself is speaking' (1963, p. 638). In mimesis, on the other hand, the poet tries to create the illusion that it is not he who speaks. Thus dialogue, monologue, direct speech in general would be mimetic, whereas indirect speech would be diegetic (a conclusion supported by the subsequent conversion of a Homeric scene of pure dialogue into diegesis). The use of both terms in this book of the *Republic* should be distinguished from other meanings attributed to them in various stages in the history of poetics. 'Mimesis', used by Socrates in the narrow sense of the direct rendering of speech, has come to designate the capacity of literature to represent or 'imitate' reality (a broad sense which can already be found in Book Ten of the *Republic*).[1] 'Diegesis', referring here to the indirect rendering of speech, was divorced by some modern narratologists (e.g. Metz 1968; Genette 1972) from the act of narration and made to designate the abstracted succession of events (my 'story').

In the *Poetics*, Aristotle (who is concerned with drama, not with narrative) does not confine 'mimesis' to the representation of speech but includes in it the notion of 'an imitation of an action' (1951, p. 34). Used in this broad sense, 'mimesis' is made to encompass diegesis as one of its types, and the original Platonic opposition is somewhat neutralized. Without engaging in a discussion of the various possible meanings of 'an imitation of an action', it is sufficient for my purpose to point out that on stage there are characters (actors) who act, make gestures and speak, in a way analogous to people's behaviour in reality. In narrative, on the other hand, all actions and gestures are rendered in words, and consequently, as we shall see later, 'an imitation of an action' becomes a more problematic concept in it.

The polarization of diegesis and mimesis reappears under the names of 'telling' and 'showing' or 'summary' and 'scene' in Anglo-American criticism of the end of the last century and the beginning of this. 'Showing' is the supposedly direct presentation of events and conversations, the narrator seeming to disappear (as in drama) and the reader being left to draw his own conclusions from what he 'sees' and 'hears'. 'Telling', on the other hand, is a presentation mediated by the narrator who, instead of directly and dramatically exhibiting events and conversations, talks about them, sums them up, etc.

Drawing inspiration from Henry James's famous injunction 'Dramatize, dramatize!' (e.g. 1962, p. 265. Orig. publ. 1907–9), Perry Lubbock erected showing into the highest ideal to which narrative fiction should aspire: 'The art of fiction does not begin until the novelist thinks of his story as a matter to be shown, to be so exhibited that it will tell itself' (1963, p.62. Orig. publ. 1921). On the basis of this norm, he attacks novelists like Fielding, Thackeray and Dickens whose narrators tell, sum up and comment. In the last twenty years the pendulum has swung back to telling, and Booth's *The Rhetoric of Fiction* (1961) is to a great extent a defence of this method and a rejection of what he considers an extreme and therefore distorting interpretation of James by Lubbock.

However interesting this normative debate is, it is ultimately irrelevant for a theoretical and descriptive study of narrative fiction. From this point of view, there is no thing inherently good or bad in either telling or showing. Like any other technique, each has its advantages and disadvantages, and their relative success or failure depends on their functionality in the given work.

THE PROBLEM OF MIMESIS

Moreover, as I have suggested earlier, the very notion of 'showing' is more problematic than it seems to be for the Anglo-American critics discussed above. As Genette (1972, pp. 185–6) argues, no text of narrative fiction can show or imitate the action it conveys, since all such texts are made of language, and language signifies without imitating. Language can only imitate language, which is why the representation of speech comes closest to pure mimesis, but even here – I believe (see p. 52) – there is a narrator who 'quotes' the characters' speech, thus reducing the directness of 'showing'. All that a narrative can do is create an illusion, an effect, a semblance of mimesis, but it does so through diegesis (in the Platonic sense). The crucial distinction, therefore, is not between telling and showing, but between different degrees and kinds of telling.[2]

How do narrative texts create the illusion of mimesis? It is convenient to start the discussion with the verbal transcription of non-verbal events. Compare 'John was angry with his wife' with 'John looked at his wife, his eyebrows pursed, his lips contracted, his fists clenched. Then he got up, banged the door and left the house'. The second account is more 'dramatic', more vivid than the first, because it gives more detailed information, reduces the narrator's role to that of a 'camera', and leaves the anger to be inferred by the reader. Thus the illusion of an imitation of events is achieved by supplying the maximum of information and the minimum of informant (Genette 1972, p. 187). Since the quantity of information was discussed under 'duration' (chapter 4, p. 54), and the presence of the narrator under 'degrees of perceptibility' (chapter 7, pp. 96–100), nothing significantly new remains to be said from this perspective about the creation of 'actional mimesis'. Let us therefore turn to the presentation of speech and its various degrees of mimetic illusion.

TYPES OF SPEECH PRESENTATION

A progressive scale, ranging from the 'purely' diegetic to the 'purely' mimetic is suggested in McHale (1978, pp. 258–9, see also Page, 1973, pp. 31–5), and I reproduce it almost verbatim, together with his examples from Dos Passos's trilogy, *U.S.A.* (1938):

1 *Diegetic summary*: The bare report that a speech act has occurred, without any specification of what was said or how it was said, e.g.:

> When Charley got a little gin inside him he started telling war yarns for the first time in his life.
>
> (*The Big Money*, p. 295)

2 *Summary, less 'purely' diegetic*: Summary which to some degree represents, not merely mentions, a speech event in that it names the topics of conversation:

> He stayed till late in the evening telling them about miraculous conversions of unbelievers, extreme unction on the firing line, a vision of the young Christ he'd seen walking among the wounded in a dressingstation during a gas attack.
>
> (*Nineteen-Nineteen*, p. 219)

3 *Indirect content paraphrase (or: Indirect discourse)*: A paraphrase of the content of a speech event, ignoring the style or form of the supposed 'original' utterance, e.g.:

> The waiter told him that Carranza's troops had lost Torreón and that Villa and Zapata were closing in on the Federal District.
>
> (*The 42nd Parallel*, p. 320)

4 *Indirect discourse, mimetic to some degree*: A form of indirect discourse which creates the illusion of 'preserving' or 'reproducing' aspects of the style of an utterance, above and beyond the mere report of its content, e.g.:

> When they came out Charley said by heck he thought he wanted to go
> up to Canada and enlist and go over and see the Great War.
>
> *(The 42nd Parallel*, p. 385)

5 *Free indirect discourse*: Grammatically and mimetically intermediate between indirect and direct discourse (more about this type will be said in the following section), e.g.:

> Why the hell shouldn't they know, weren't they off'n her and out to see
> the goddam town and he'd better come along.
>
> *(Nineteen-Nineteen*, pp. 43–4)

6 *Direct discourse*: A 'quotation' of a monologue or a dialogue. This creates the illusion of 'pure' mimesis, although it is always stylized in one way or another, e.g.:

> Fred Summers said, 'Fellers, this war's the most gigantic cockeyed
> graft of the century and me for it and the cross red nurses [sic]'.
>
> *(Nineteen-Nineteen*, p. 191)

7 *Free direct discourse*: Direct discourse shorn of its conventional orthographic cues. This is the typical form of first-person interior monologue, e.g.:

> Fainy's head suddenly got very light. Bright boy, that's me, ambition
> and literary taste. . . . Gee, I must finish *Looking Backward*. . . and jez, I
> like reading fine, an' I could run a linotype or set up print if anybody'd
> let me. Fifteen bucks a week . . . pretty soft, ten dollars' raise.
>
> *(The 42nd Parallel*, p. 22. Dos Passos's suspension points)

FREE INDIRECT DISCOURSE

Among the seven degrees of speech presentation, the one that has recently given rise to a proliferation of studies on the part of both linguists and narrative theorists is free indirect discourse[3] (see, for example, Banfield 1973, 1978a, 1978b, 1981; Bronzwaer 1970; Cohn 1966, 1978; Hernadi 1971, 1972; Kuroda 1973; McHale 1978; Page

1972, 1973; Pascal 1962,1977; Perry forthcoming; Ron 1981).[4] Therefore, in spite of its being only one form of rendering speech, I propose to devote some space to it separately, briefly describing the main linguistic features of FID, its most common functions, and its special status within poetics.

It should be noted from the start that although the 'orthodox' view limits FID to a linguistic combination of two voices, many theorists consider the phenomenon to be only partly linguistic. Thus Golomb (1968, pp. 251–62) discusses, under what he calls 'combined speech', not only the co-presence of two voices but also that of the narrator's voice and a character's pre-verbal perception or feeling. Bal (1981) subsumes the phenomenon under her concept of 'embedding' which she sees operating between two utterances, two focalizations, or an utterance and a focalization. Perry (forthcoming) is perhaps the most extreme in enlarging the scope of the phenomenon:

> Combined Discourse is formed when together with a basic frame of discourse an alternative, secondary frame is activated, which organizes some of the elements. The frame is not the formal or official linguistic frame; it has other indicators – linguistic or thematic – and once constructed, is always incongruent with the formal frame.

For him, FID is only a part of a more comprehensive phenomenon, i.e. alternative patternings which are activated in the reading process. However, in my study, under the heading of 'narration', a narrower concept than Perry's is more relevant. The cognate aspects are discussed under 'focalization' (chapter 6) and 'the text and its reading' (chapter 9).

Linguistic features

The linguistic features of FID give the impression of combining direct discourse with indirect discourse, as the following list shows:[5]

1 Reporting verb of saying/thinking and conjunction 'that' DD: The reporting verb is either directly present or implied by the use of quotation marks, but the reported utterance is not syntactically subordinate to it. The conjunction 'that' is absent (e.g. he said: 'I love her').

ID: The reporting verb always appears, subordinating the reported utterance; the conjunction 'that' is optional (but logically implied when absent e.g. He said that he loved her). FID: Deletion of reporting verb + conjunction 'that' (e.g. He loved her).

2 Tense-scheme

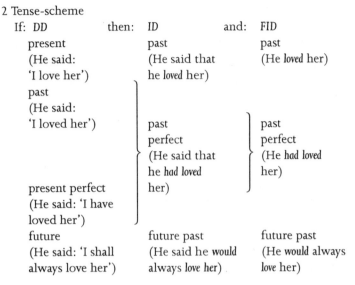

If: DD	then: ID	and: FID
present (He said: 'I love her')	past (He said that he *loved* her)	past (He *loved* her)
past (He said: 'I loved her')		
	past perfect (He said that he *had loved* her)	past perfect (He *had loved* her)
present perfect (He said: 'I have loved her')		
future (He said: 'I shall always love her')	future past (He said he *would* always *love her*)	future past (He *would* always love her)

Thus FID retains the 'back-shift' of tenses characteristic of ID.

3 Personal and possessive pronouns
If these are the first and second person in DD, they become third person in both ID and FID. ('I love her' thus becomes '*he* loved her').

4 Deictics (i.e. demonstrative expressions)

DD	ID	FID
now (He said: 'I live in Jerusalem now')	then (He said he lived in Jerusalem then)	now (He lives in Jerusalem now)
today	that day	today
tomorrow	the next day	tomorrow
here	there	here

Thus FID preserves the deictic elements of DD.

5 Questions

DD	ID	FID
Verb + Subject	Subject + Verb	Verb + Subject
(She asked: 'Do	(She asked if	(as in DD)
you love me?')	he loved her)	(Did he love
		her?)

6 Vocatives, interjections, lexical registers or dialectical features

DD	ID	FID
Admissible	Inadmissible	Admissible

To sum up in McHale's words, FID 'resembles ID in person and tense, while it resembles DD in not being strictly subordinate to a 'higher' verb of saying/thinking, and in deictic elements, the word-order of questions, and the admissibility of various DD features' (1978, p. 252).

Functions

In specific fictional texts FID can have a variety of thematic functions, contributing or being analogous to the governing thematic principle(s) of the work under consideration. Thus Bronzwaer (1970) shows how it conveys the theme of the discontinuous, developing self in a novel by Iris Murdoch. Similarly McHale (1978) sees FID as enacting and imaging the modes of determinism in Dos Passos. However, such functions vary from text to text or from corpus to corpus, and are not easily amenable to generalization. The functions with which I am concerned here, on the other hand, are more general, and each of them may have varying thematic manifestations in different fictional texts.

1 The FID hypothesis (even if not thought of in these terms) is often necessary in order to identify speakers and assign given speech-features or attitudes to them. This enables the reader to make sense of 'deviant' linguistic practices, unacceptable attitudes, or even lies, without undermining the credibility of the work or of the implied author (Ron 198 1, pp. 28–9).

2 Even when different segments can ultimately be attributed to identifiable speakers and more so when they cannot, FID enhances the bivocality or polyvocality of the text by bringing into play a plurality of speakers and attitudes (McHale 1978). In cases of an ambiguity concerning the speaker, it also dramatizes the problematic relationship between any utterance and its origin. This function is, at least in some sense, opposed to the first, a contrast resulting from the double-edged effect characteristic of FID.

3 The plurality of speakers and attitudes, the co-existence of what Perry calls 'alternative patternings', contributes to the semantic density of the text (forthcoming).

4 Because of its capacity to reproduce the idiolect of a character's speech or thought – some would add: pre-verbal perceptions, whether visual, auditory or tactile – within the narrator's reporting language, FID is a convenient vehicle for representing stream of consciousness, mainly for the variety called 'indirect interior monologue' (Banfield 1973; McHale 1978).

5 The FID hypothesis can assist the reader in reconstructing the implied author's attitude toward the character(s) involved. However, here again a double-edged effect may be noticed. On the one hand, the presence of a narrator as distinct from the character may create an ironic distancing. On the other hand, the tinting of the narrator's speech with the character's language or mode of experience may promote an empathetic identification on the part of the reader (Ewen 1968; McHale 1978; and many others). Perhaps most interesting are cases of ambiguity, where the reader has no means of choosing between the ironic and the empathetic attitude.

Status within poetics

The peculiar interest in FID evinced by contemporary narrative theory is due not only to its stylistic complexity but also to its constituting, in some sense, a miniature reflection of the nature of both mimesis (in the broad sense of representation) and literariness.

The concept of FID is meaningful only within mimesis (in the broad sense) (Ron 1981), because the need to attribute textual segments to speakers as well as the urge to account for apparently false statements and reconcile seeming contradictions exists only when the text is grasped as in some sense analogous to (mimetic of) reality. A non-mimetic text would tend to play havoc with such attributions; in it, as Barthes says, 'the discourse, or better, the language, speaks: nothing more' (1974, p. 41. Orig. publ. 1970). There is therefore no sense in constructing an FID hypothesis in order to arrive at an unnecessary and at best partial recuperation of the origin of utterances.

If FID loses the status of a specific phenomenon in non-mimetic texts, it paradoxically gains the status of a miniature reflection of the nature of all texts and all language. For language, as Derrida has repeatedly argued (e.g. 1967, 1977), always 'quotes' other language, constituting itself on linguistic iterability and cultural clichés whose direct utterers are nowhere present. From this point of view, all language becomes – in operation if not in grammatical form – a kind of free indirect discourse (for a more detailed discussion of the whole issue, see Ron 1981, pp. 17–18, 36–8).

Whereas 'mimesis' names a relationship between literature and a certain version of reality, 'literariness' designates the specifically literary (non-referential) aspect of literature (see Hawkes 1977, pp. 71–3 for a discussion of the notion of literariness). And just as FID is often seen to index mimesis, so – at the other pole – it can be grasped as marking literariness. In a relatively weak sense, FID marks literariness simply by figuring more frequently and centrally in literature than in other forms of discourse. It is perhaps because of the difficulty a speaker would experience in trying to perform orally the co-presence of voices characteristic of FID that the phenomenon seems more congenial to the silent register of writing (McHale 1978, pp. 282–3, following Voloshinov 1973. Orig. publ. in Russian 1930). And although FID is by no means exclusively literary, it is at least characteristic enough of literature or fiction to have a fictional ring even when found in other types of discourse (Bronzwaer 1970, p. 49).

In a stronger – non-statistical – sense, FID marks literariness by being a paradigm, a kind of *mise en abyme* of what some theoreticians consider a principal characteristic of narrative fiction. According to Bakhtin (1973. Orig. publ. in Russian 1929), the central tradition of the novel is constituted by texts which are not unitary in their discourse ('monological') but multiple, polyphonic ('dialogic'). This polyphonic quality is achieved both by the juxtaposition of several voices in the text itself and by the text's integration of previous discourse, be it anterior literary texts or aspects of language and culture at large. From this perspective, FID seems like a formal mirroring of the larger, 'trans-linguistic' phenomenon.[6] The co-existence of various voices in it creates intra-textual polyphony, while the preservation of the linguistic register of the speaker orients the utterance toward previous ones, thereby creating inter-textual polyphony. However, from the Derridian viewpoint glimpsed above, it may be argued that the citational quality of FID, being common to all language, deprives this phenomenon as well as the whole of literature of its privileged differential status. Once again FID reveals its double-edged nature, a double-edgedness which is itself characteristic of many phenomena in literature.

9

THE TEXT AND ITS READING

THE ROLE OF THE READER

'How to produce texts by reading them' – this title of a section in Eco's book (1979, p. 3) is an extreme formulation of a tendency that has become more and more pronounced during the last ten or fifteen years.[1] Whereas the Anglo-American New Critics and the French Structuralists treated the text as a more or less autonomous object, the new orientation stresses the reciprocal relations between text and reader:

> a text can only come to life when it is read, and if it is to be examined, it must therefore be studied through the eyes of the reader.
>
> (Iser 1971b, pp. 2–3)

The written text is conceived of as having a virtual dimension which calls for the reader's construction of the unwritten text (Iser 1974, p. 31). This virtuality contributes to the dynamic character of the reading process and gives the reader a certain degree of freedom (but only a certain degree, since the written text does exercise some control over the process).

Just as the reader participates in the production of the text's meaning so the text shapes the reader. On the one hand it 'selects' its appropriate reader, projects an image of such a reader, through its specific linguistic code, its style, the 'encyclopedia' it implicitly presupposes (Eco 1979, p. 7). On the other hand, just as the text pre-shapes a certain competence to be brought by the reader from the outside, so in the course of reading, it develops in the reader a specific competence needed to come to grips with it, often inducing him to change his previous conceptions and modify his outlook. The reader is thus both an image of a certain competence brought to the text and a structuring of such a competence within the text.

The philosophical influence behind most reader-oriented approaches is phenomenology, more specifically Ingarden's application of Husserl's theory to literature (1973. Orig. publ. in Polish 1931). Ingarden distinguishes between autonomous and heteronomous objects. While autonomous objects have immanent (i.e. indwelling, inherent) properties only, heteronomous ones are characterized by a combination of immanent properties and properties attributed to them by consciousness. Thus heteronomous objects do not have a full existence without the participation of consciousness, without the activation of a subject–object relationship. Since literature belongs to this category, it requires 'concretization' or 'realization' by a reader.

In this chapter I shall present some contributions of the phenomenology of reading to the poetics of narrative fiction. However, in spite of this new slant, the focus of the chapter (as its title implies) will remain the text. Thus the analysis will modify a few structuralist assumptions, but will not represent the more far-reaching 'revisionism' of some reader-oriented studies, because that is often at odds with the very project of narrative poetics. Moreover, I shall concentrate mainly on those aspects of the reader–text interaction which are specific to narrative fiction. Problems like the reader's response or the formation of attitudes will therefore not be discussed in detail, except when they are influenced by the 'temporal' unfolding of both story and text which characterizes narrative fiction.

Recurrent references have been made in the foregoing pages to the reading process and the role of the reader, but who is the reader I am talking about? Is he the 'Actual Reader' (Van Dijk, Jauss), the 'Super-reader' (Riffaterre), the 'Informed Reader' (Fish), the 'Ideal Reader' (Culler), the 'Model Reader' (Eco), the 'Implied Reader' (Booth, Iser,

Chatman, Perry), or the 'Encoded Reader' (Brooke-Rose)? An analysis of the similarities and differences among the concepts underlying this plethora of appelations would take me far beyond the specificity of narrative fiction. It is sufficient for my purpose to point out that the list yields two diametrically opposed views and various nuances between them. At one extreme the concept is of a real reader, whether a specific individual or the collective readership of a period. At the other, it is a theoretical construct, implied or encoded in the text, representing the integration of data and the interpretative process 'invited' by the text.

It should be clear from my declared focus that the 'reader' is seen in this book as a construct, a 'metonymic characterization of the text' (Perry 1979, p.43), an 'it' rather than a personified 'he' or 'she' (see also chapter 7).[2] Such a reader is 'implied' or 'encoded' in the text 'in the very rhetoric through which he is required to "make sense of the content" or reconstruct it "as a world" ' (Brooke-Rose 1908b, p. 160). Consequently, the relevance of the psychology of readers is fairly limited, but a few psychological observations which bear directly on the dynamics of reading inscribed in the text will be included in the next section. The advantage of talking of an implied reader rather than of 'textual strategies' pure and simple (as Doležel does, 1980, p. 182) is that it implies a view of the text as a system of reconstruction-inviting structures rather than as an autonomous object. A re-perusal of the previous chapters can show that a reader of this kind was implicit in many of them. Thus analepses are often used to provide information necessary to the reader and prolepses to arouse the reader's expectations, the story is abstracted by the reader, and characters are constructed by the reader from various indications dispersed along the text-continuum. What was only implied in the previous chapters will be discussed directly in this.

THE DYNAMICS OF READING

As stated in chapter 4, language prescribes a linear figuration of signs and hence a linear presentation of information about things. Not only does it dictate a progression from letter to letter, word to word, sentence to sentence, etc., it also imposes upon the reader a successive perception of bits of information even when these are meant to be understood as simultaneous in the story. This may seem to some an unfortunate limitation of language, in comparison to painting (for example) or to double-exposure effects in the cinema. However, narrative texts (and literature in general) can make a virtue of necessity and obtain various rhetorical effects from the linear nature of the medium. The text can direct and control the reader's comprehension and attitudes by positioning *certain* items before others. Perry (1979, p. 53) sums up the results of psychological tests which have shown the crucial influence of initial information on the process of perception ('primary effect'). Thus, information and attitudes presented at an early stage of the text tend to encourage the reader to interpret everything in their light. The reader is prone to preserve such meanings and attitudes for as long as possible. For example, in Tolstoy's *Anna Karenina* (1873–76), the reader's initial impression of Anna lingers long after the less pleasant aspects of her character are seen to dominate her behaviour. Texts can encourage the reader's tendency to comply with the primacy effect by constantly reinforcing the initial impressions, but on the whole they induce the reader to modify or replace the original conjectures. 'The literary text, then, *exploit* the "powers" of the primacy effect, but ordinarily it sets up a mechanism to oppose them, giving rise, rather, to a *recency* effect' (Perry 1979, p. 57). The recency effect encourages the reader to assimilate all previous information to the item presented last. In Patrick White's *The Solid Mandala* (1966), for example, Arthur is seen in the first half of the novel through the eyes of his twin brother, as limited in intelligence and incapable of interpreting the world around him. This view, however, is followed by a presentation of Arthur as a sensitive, intuitive, artist-cum-Christ figure in the last part, narrated through his own perception. Although the 'correct' view is a subtle combination of both presentations, the reader tends to reject the former in favour of the latter.

Thus, placing an item at the beginning or at the end may radically change the process of reading as well as the final product. Interestingly, as could be glimpsed from the examples given above, both the primacy and the recency effects may be so strong as to overshadow the meanings and attitudes which would have emerged from a full and consistent integration of the data of the text. Linearity can also be exploited to arouse suspense or deliberately mislead the reader by delaying various bits of information (see pp. 125–7) and this too may cause him to construct meanings which will have to be revised at a later stage.

The reader, we have seen, does not wait until the end to understand the text. Although texts provide information only gradually, they encourage the reader to start integrating data from the very beginning (Perry 1979, p. 47). From this perspective, reading can be seen as a continuous process of forming hypotheses, reinforcing them, developing them, modifying them, and sometimes replacing them by others or dropping them altogether. It should be noted, however, that even rejected hypotheses may continue exercising some influence on the reader's comprehension.

By the end of the reading process, the reader usually will have reached a 'finalized hypothesis', an overall meaning which makes sense of the text as a whole. The degree of 'finalization' varies from text to text. In detective novels the end discloses a definitive solution to the problem which the narrative set out to solve: X is the murderer, Y is the thief, Z's death was caused by fire. But sometimes the reader closes a book without a definitive solution. This may be caused by the co-existence of a few 'finalized' hypotheses which either complement each other in some way (multiple meaning) or mutually exclude each other without providing grounds for deciding between them (narrative ambiguity) (Rimmon 1977, p. 10. See also Perry and Sternberg 1968b, by which the above was partly influenced). Thus at the end of James's 'The Figure in the Carpet' (1896) the reader cannot decide between hypothesis (1) 'there is a figure in Vereker's carpet' and hypothesis (2) 'there is no figure in Vereker's carpet'. Instead of closure there is perpetual oscillation between two possibilities. Some texts (mainly modern) seem designed so as to prevent the formation of any 'finalized hypothesis' or overall meaning by making various items undermine each other or cancel each other out, without forming neatly opposed possibilities. This phenomenon, highly cherished by post-structuralists (or deconstructionists), is referred to as 'undecid-ability' or 'unreadability' and taken to be characteristic of literature at large (see, for example, Miller 1980, pp. 107–18, and the debate with Rimmon-Kenan, 1980/81, pp. 185–91).

The progressive integration of information often requires a retro-spective patterning of earlier parts of the text. Such reconsideration can take one of two forms: (1) A further utilization of the past, reinforcing or developing it without contradicting or cancelling its previous meanings or effects. For example, with every incident involving the possibility of arson in Faulkner's 'Barn Burning' (1939), the reader will go back to previous incidents in order to accumulate all the details which may explain the father's motivation. (2) A re-examination of the past which modifies, transforms, or rejects its previous meanings or effects. Thus at the end of Faulkner's 'A Rose for Emily' (1930) the smell incident is reconstructed and is now clearly linked with the corpse lying upstairs for forty years, not with a rat or a snake killed by either Emily or her servant, as an earlier stage of the text led the reader to believe. The first form of retrospective reconstruction involves only *additional* patterning; it preserves consistency and is therefore preferable as long as it is possible. The second form, on the other hand, effects a complete repatterning and often causes surprise or shock (Perry 1979, pp. 59–60).

In addition to harking back to the past, reading also involves 'leaps' into the future, the reader often hazarding various guesses as to what 'is going to happen' in the sequel. The past is now assimilated to the future, and the reader waits to see whether his expectations will or will not be fulfilled. When they are, the effect is one of satisfaction but also of a lulling of interest. When they are not, a sharp confrontation between the expected and the actual ensues, and this leads to an active re-examination and modification of the past.[3]

THE PARADOXICAL POSITION OF THE TEXT *VIS-À-VIS* ITS READER

There is one end every text must achieve: it must make certain that it will be read; its very existence, as it were, depends on it. Interestingly, the text is caught here in a double bind. On the one hand, in order to be read it must make itself understood, it must enhance intelligibility by anchoring itself in codes, frames, *Gestalten* familiar to the reader. But if the text is understood too quickly, it would thereby come to an untimely end. So, on the other hand, it is in the text's interest to slow down the process of comprehension by the reader so as to ensure its own survival. To this end, it will introduce unfamiliar elements, it will multiply difficulties of one kind or another (Shklovsky 1965, p. 12. Orig. publ. in Russian 1917), or simply delay the presentation of expected, interesting items.[4]

Intelligibility, or how the reader makes sense of the text?

Making sense of a text requires an integration of its elements with each other, an integration which involves an appeal to various familiar models of coherence (Culler 1975, p. 159). The assimilation of the text to *déjà-vu* models is called 'naturalization' by Culler: 'to naturalize a text is to bring it into relation with a type of discourse or model which is already, in some sense, natural and legible' (1975, p. 138).[5] These already-natural-and-legible models have been variously called 'codes' in Barthes (1970), *'Gestalten'* in Iser (1971a), 'frames of reference' in Hrushovski (1976), 'intertextual frames' in Eco (1 979) and 'frames' *tout court* in Perry (1979). In spite of differences in detail, the underlying concepts seem to me similar. Compare, for example, Culler's definition quoted above with Barthes's description of the codes:

> The code is a perspective of quotations, a mirage of structures . . . so many fragments of something that has always been *already* read, seen, done, experienced; the code is the wake of that *already*.
>
> (1974, p. 20. Orig. publ. in French 1970)

Even closer to Culler (though not influenced by him) is Perry's formulation: 'This construction of the reading process on the basis of models with which the reader is familiar is a use of a *set of frames*' (1979, p. 36. His emphasis) which can be chronological, spatial, formal, linguistic, logical, pseudo-logical, etc.

To use a frame, it seems to me, is to ground a hypothesis in a *déjà-vu* model of coherence (or, put differently, to form a hypothesis by reference to such a model). The dynamics of reading can thus be seen not only as a formation, development, modification, and replacement of hypotheses (see p. 121), but also – simultaneously – as the construction of frames, their transformation, and dismantling. Like Culler, Perry also relates the construction of hypotheses to the integration of data:

any reading of a text is a process of constructing a system of hypotheses or frames which can create maximal relevancy among the various data of the text – which can motivate their 'co-presence' in the text according to models derived from 'reality', from literary or cultural conventions, and the like. Each of these hypotheses is a sort of 'label' constituting an answer to questions such as: What is happening? What is the state of affairs? What is the situation? Where is this happening? What are the motives? What is the purpose? What is the speaker's position? What is the argument or the idea 'reflected' in the text? And so on.

(1979, p. 43)

'Models of coherence' can derive either from 'reality' or from literature.[6] Reality models help naturalize elements by reference to some concept (or structure) which governs our perception of the world. Such models of coherence can be so familiar that they seem natural and are hardly grasped as models. Chronology and causality belong to this category (and see chapter 4 for a comment on their pseudo-naturalness). Barthes's code of action ('proairetic code') is based on this type of model which tells us, for example, that a ringing phone can either be answered or ignored, or that a baby cannot be born before his mother got pregnant. Contiguity in space is another seemingly natural model. On the other hand, there are reality models which are not grasped as natural but rather recognized by the given society as generalizations or stereotypes, 'a body of maxims and prejudices which constitute a vision of the world and a system of values' (Genette 1969, pp. 73–5, translated by Culler 1975, p. 144). Barthes's 'cultural' code belongs to this category, and a generalization like 'modest women blush' thus helps the reader interpret 'Zambinella blushes' (in Balzac's *Sarrasine*, 1830) as 'Zambinella is a woman'.[7]

Unlike reality models, literature models do not involve a mediation through some concept of the world. Rather they make elements intelligible by reference to specifically literary exigencies or institutions. An element may thus be accounted for in terms of its contribution to the action (Hamlet does not kill Claudius in Act I scene 1, because this would have been the end of the play), or its illustration of a theme (the heroine's house in Faulkner's 'A Rose for Emily' is described as decaying in order to evoke the degeneration of the South), or the like. A more institutionalized literary model is genre. Its conventions establish a kind of contract between the text and the reader, so that some expectations are rendered plausible, others ruled out, and elements which would seem strange in another context are made intelligible within the genre (Culler 1975 p. 147). Thus a human being flying in the air can be made intelligible and acceptable if the text belongs to the genre of the Marvellous (on the Marvellous, see Todorov 1970).

Self-survival, or how the text 'tempts' the reader to continue reading

Although everything in a text can ultimately be naturalized, made intelligible, either by reality models or by models derived from literature, the text's very existence depends on maintaining the phase of the 'not yet fully known or intelligible' for as long as possible. Narrative texts implicitly keep promising the reader the great prize of understanding – later. They suggest, with varying degrees of subtlety: 'the best is yet to come, don't stop reading now, thus stimulating interest, curiosity or suspense. In this section I shall examine two ways of slowing down comprehension and creating suspense: delay and gaps.

Delay

Delay consists in not imparting information where it is 'due' in the text, but leaving it for a later stage. Depending on the temporal dimension to which the withheld information belongs, delay can create suspense of two different types: future-oriented and past-oriented (i.e. oriented toward the future or the past of the story). The future-oriented type consists in keeping alive the question 'what next?' (and is thus related to Barthes's proairetic code). This need not involve any temporal displacement; events may be narrated in the order in which they are supposed to have occurred. But they must be events of the kind which will arouse a strong expectation for the continuation of the sequence, coupled with a strong uncertainty as to *how* it should continue (e.g. the hero's life is in danger, there is a struggle which can end in the victory of either side, a difficult and complicated plan is being put into execution, etc.). In order to increase the reader's interest and prolong itself, the text will delay the narration of the next event in the story, or of the event the reader is now curious to learn about, or of the event which will temporarily or permanently close off the sequence in question. Thus in Fielding's *Joseph Andrews*, the narrator interrupts the story of the kidnapping of Fanny and instead of telling the final outcome – will the sequence end in rescue or in rape? – introduces a digression: 'A discourse between the poet and the player; of no other use in this history but to divert the reader' (1962, p. 203. Orig. publ. 1742). The reader, in fact, does not want to be diverted. He would much rather learn about Fanny's fate, and he is thus held in suspense.

The past-oriented delay consists in keeping alive questions like 'what happened?' 'who did it?', 'why?', 'what is the meaning of all this?' Here story-time may go on, but the reader's comprehension of the narrated events is impeded by the omission of information (i.e. the creation of a gap) about the past or the present. For example, in Le Carré's *The Spy Who Came In from the Cold* (1963) the reader is not informed until almost the end of the book that the efforts of the British agent, Leamas, to bring down the East German intelligence officer, Mundt, are part of a scheme devised by Mundt and by Leamas's own superiors, unknown to him, to discredit another East German officer.

Delay thus turns the reading process (or one of its aspects) into a guessing game, an attempt to solve a riddle or a puzzle. As Barthes has shown in his analysis of what he calls 'the hermeneutic code', this game is structured by various units which need not all appear in every text. The first stages are marking the enigmatic object ('thematization' of the enigma), suggesting the existence of an enigma concerning this object ('position' of the enigma), formulating it, and at least implicitly promising an answer. Following the introduction of the enigma, the text establishes a paradoxical process, akin to the one I have sketched earlier: on the one hand, it seems to be pushing toward a solution, while on the other it endeavours to maintain the enigma as long as possible in order to secure its own existence. It thus introduces various retardatory devices, such as snare (misleading clue), equivocation, blockage, suspended answer, partial answer (Barthes 1970, pp. 80–1, 215–16).

Whether the delay is future-oriented or past-oriented, the various retardatory devices can be naturalized by reference to either literature models or reality models, or – to use the Formalist terms which seem appropriate here – they can be either artistically or realistically motivated. Fielding's delay through the narrator's digression, reflecting upon the purposes and effects of his narration (see p. 126), belongs to the first category. In the second category, delays are made plausible in terms of occurrences in the story itself, e.g. the death of a character who bears certain information, the departure of a character, his missing a train or losing a letter which contains crucial information, a character's refusal to divulge information out of fear, discretion, or whatnot. Henry James's 'The Figure in the Carpet' (1896) abounds in this kind of motivation (see Rimmon 1973).

Both future-oriented and past-oriented delays can be either *local*, i.e. involve only a portion or an aspect of the text (as in the above example from *Joseph Andrews*) or *global*, i.e. effect a major portion of the text or its entirety (as in detective novels or in 'The Figure in the Carpet').

Gaps

How to make a bagel? First you take a hole. . . . And how to make a narrative text? In exactly the same way. Holes or gaps are so central in narrative fiction because the materials the text provides for the reconstruction of a world (or a story) are insufficient for saturation. No matter how detailed the presentation is, further questions can always be asked; gaps always remain open. 'No tale', says Iser,

> can be told in its entirety. Indeed, it is only through inevitable omissions that a story will gain its dynamism. Thus whenever the flow is interrupted and we are led off in unexpected directions, the opportunity is given to us to bring into play our own faculty for establishing connections – for filling in gaps left by the text itself.
>
> (1971, p. 285)

As we have seen above, the integration of information dispersed in the text and thus also the filling-in of gaps is effected by reference to models of coherence, or frames. Thus Perry: 'The selection of any particular frame leads *ipso facto* to supplying information (filling gaps) which has no direct verbal basis in the text' (1979, p. 45). But the choice of frames can also create gaps, both because the frames themselves cannot be saturated, and because clashes between them may give rise to further questions.

The most typical gap in narrative fiction is the hermeneutic (also called 'information gap'). Early studies (e.g. Perry and Sternberg 1968b, pp. 263–93 and Rimmon 1977, pp. 45–58) tended to concentrate on this species in its own right. Later studies (e.g. Perry 1979; Eco 1979) integrate them within the larger process of frame-selection, modification, and replacement. The hermeneutic aspect of reading consists in detecting an enigma (a gap), searching for clues, forming hypotheses, trying to choose among them and (more often than not) constructing one finalized hypothesis.

Hermeneutic gaps can range from very trivial ones, which are either filled-in automatically (Daisy Miller appears at the hotel, therefore she must have been born; Beardsley 1958, p. 242) or do not require filling-in (many gaps in the Bible), through various degrees of importance, to gaps which are so crucial and central in the narrative as to become the very pivot of the reading process ('Who done it?' in detective stories, 'Are there or are there not real ghosts at Bly?' in James's *The Turn of the Screw*).

Regardless of the centrality of the gap, it can be either *temporary*, i.e. filled-in at some point in the text (as in most detective stories), or *permanent*, i.e. remain open even after the text has come to an end (as in *The Turn of the Screw*). The distinction between temporary and permanent gaps can be made only in retrospect. In the process of reading, the reader cannot know whether a gap is temporary or permanent; indeed this uncertainty is at the basis of the dynamics of reading.

Temporary gaps result from a discrepancy between story-time and text-time. We have already seen that a past-oriented delay necessarily involves a gap. A prolepsis may also create a gap by leaving out various stages between the first narrative and the predicted future. An analepsis, on the other hand, often fills-in an anterior gap, but it may also create a new gap by giving a different slant to already-narrated events, thus making it difficult to reconcile fresh impressions with 'old' ones. Created by temporal displacements, such gaps exist in the text alone. In the abstracted story the withheld information will appear in its appropriate place in the chronology. Permanent gaps, on the other hand, exist in both story and text: the information is never given. Thus a gap in the story entails a gap in the text, but a gap in the text need not entail a corresponding gap in the story.

The reader may or may not be made aware of the existence of a gap in the process of reading. When he is, the gap is *prospective*, and the reading-process becomes (at least partly) an attempt to fill it in. But sometimes a text can prevent the reader from asking the right question until it is answered. The gap, in this case, is *retrospective*. In Dickens's *Great Expectations*, for example, the question 'Who is Pip's secret benefactor?' is not seriously asked until the solution is provided by the events themselves. Only after the fact does the reader realize that some significant information has been withheld from him.

Whatever category the gap belongs to, it always enhances interest and curiosity, prolongs the reading process, and contributes to the reader's dynamic participation in making the text signify.

10

CONCLUSION

Has this book been an introduction to or an obituary of the poetics of narrative fiction? Both reactions are possible, yet neither seems to me quite adequate. In many circles, including some universities, the poetics of narrative fiction is either ignored or treated with suspicion. For them, this book can serve as an introduction. In other circles, this discipline is already considered dead or at least superseded by deconstruction. From their point of view this book would be an obituary. And yet the poetics of narrative fiction is neither the newborn babe it may seem to the former nor the corpse it may seem to the latter. The discipline is still alive and kicking, although (or perhaps because) it no longer enjoys the privilege of the latest fashion. Moreover, it seems to me that deconstruction may, perhaps in spite of its self, contribute to the poetics of narrative fiction rather than undermine it. It is with such an optimistic suggestion that I would like to conclude.

Among other things, deconstruction challenges the notion of *differentia specifica* which was central to my presentation (see chapter 1, pp. 1–3, 5). Instead of distinguishing between narrative fiction and other types of narrative (as I have tried to do), deconstruction is interested precisely in the elements shared by novels, films, comic strips, dance, news reports, history books, psychoanalytic sessions and philosophical discussions – cultural products traditionally classified as non-verbal, non-fictional, or non-narrative. As shown in chapter 2, narratology also deals with a common denominator of various types of narrative. This common denominator is found to be the 'story' – a non-verbal construct which narratology abstracts from the verbal text as well as from other sign-systems. Deconstruction, on the other hand, is interested in the verbal, rather than non-verbal, similarities between all types of narrative. Instead of abstracting a common, 'pre-medium' aspect from various narratives, it investigates narrative elements in the very rhetoric of historical, philosophical, and psychoanalytic texts (see, for example, Derrida 1967a, 1967b, 1972; de Man 1971, 1979; Lacan 1966; Felman 1977; Brooks 1977, 1979; Chase 1979; Norris 1982). Because of their tendency to draw attention to their own rhetoricity and fictionality, literary narratives become a kind of paradigm, used to unearth narrative elements in texts where such consciousness is usually less explicit. Seen in this way, the study of narrative is no longer restricted to poetics but becomes an attempt to describe fundamental operations of any signifying system.

These are exciting and promising developments, not least (from the point of view of poetics) because they 'make possible productive investigations of the relationship between literature and other modes of ordering and representing experience' (Culler 1981, p. 215). However, they are often considered incompatible with the poetics of narrative fiction. This is so, because their emphasis on narrative elements in texts traditionally classified as non-narrative as well as their tracing of fictionality in so-called non-fictional texts seems to do away with 'narrative fiction' as a separate category. Nevertheless, it may be argued that awareness of the presence of narrative and fictional elements in supposedly non-narrative and non-fictional texts need not cancel the *differentia specifica* of narrative fiction. On the contrary, with this new awareness it is possible to re-examine each type of narrative separately and discover new differences within the similarities. To be sure, these differences may not be the ones isolated by poetics so far, but this is only to the good. Coping with the challenge represented by the new perspective, poetics will be able to advance its own understanding of narrative fiction by posing again 'the question of the distinctiveness of literature while also demonstrating the centrality of literary structures to the organization of experience' (Culler 1981, p. 215). This kind of spiralling movement, envisaged by Eliot in a completely different context, will hopefully keep us all on the move:

> We shall not cease from exploration
> And the end of all our exploring
> Will be to arrive where we started
> And know the place for the first time.
>   ('Little Gidding' in *Four Quartets*)

11

TOWARDS . . .

Afterthoughts, almost twenty years later

STORIES OF NARRATOLOGY; THE STORY OF *NARRATIVE FICTION*

'Whatever happened to narratology?' is the provocative title of an essay by Christine Brooke-Rose (1990, p. 283). This question, asked by many in various forms since *Narrative Fiction* was published (1983), and probably also before, has itself the makings of a narrative. It revolves around a word which points to an event, perhaps the paradigm of all events – 'happened' – and its hypothetical answers are bound to include at least two, probably more, events. Thus, in terms of the theories on which *Narrative Fiction* draws, the answers are likely to be at least minimal stories.

By now we have learnt from Hayden White that there are always competing narratives, and, indeed, the trajectory of narratology can be, and has been, envisaged in many ways. Some tell the story of the rise and fall of narratology – a story consisting of two main events, its closure sometimes mitigated by the substitution of 'crisis' for 'fall' or 'death'. 'Crisis' implies the possibility of a third event: recovery, modification, shift of emphasis, or transformation. Other versions of a tripartite narrative go even further in the direction of development, constructing a story of the rise, fall, and renaissance of narratology. And still others are content with a story of continuity: narratology is a specialized discipline and, as such, it continues to be practised and amplified by a relatively limited number of specialists.

Where do I stand in relation to these narratives? The present chapter is an attempt to reconsider narratology, its presuppositions, definitions, the inclusions and exclusions these entailed, the various transformations they have undergone, and some of the new developments that have emerged from re-thinking the discipline. A reconsideration of narratology has become a genre of its own (Martin 1986, Cohan and Shires 1988, O'Neill 1994, Herman 1999, Nünning 1999), but – at the cost of limiting the scope somewhat – I wish to focus mine on assumptions most relevant to *Narrative Fiction*. To the extent that this book integrates various theories, the present re-thinking applies to narratology at large. However, to the extent that the book conveys – by its selections, exclusions and even explicit commentary – a personal position on the issues discussed, the present focus adds a personal dimension to the general exploration. Incidentally, 'a personal dimension' is also one of the signs of the times, one of the changes that occurred between the discourse used in this book and a great deal of latter-day theorizing. In this sense, I undertake a role somewhat similar to that of a retrospective first-person narrator: a fairly complex role, often entailing double focalization, never free of the danger of unreliability. I have decided to risk these dangers rather than give up the wonderful opportunity (and challenge) presented by the 25th anniversary of *New Accents*: the opportunity of putting together reflections, doubts, readings, and teaching experiences that have shaped my attitude to narratology since the publication of this book. It is perhaps best to say from the start that I have been forced to question quite a few of my assumptions. I have changed many of my views, and my work has taken various new directions. Nevertheless, I still find narratology a valuable, even indispensable enterprise. I prefer to focus this re-exploration on basic assumptions rather than on specific concepts (e.g. time, author, unreliability, homo/hetero-diegetic narration), because at this late stage in the game it seems to me more interesting and more radical.

NARRATOLOGY: ASSUMPTIONS, DEFINITIONS, EXCLUSIONS

At the time my book was written, narratology was for me (and for many others) mainly a formalist-structuralist discipline.[1] As a result, some of its assumptions were inherited from structuralism, others were more focused on the specific object of study envisaged by narratology. This duality is evident in the assumptions explicitly presented in the introduction to *Narrative Fiction*, which I shall discuss presently. The conceptual presuppositions are: 1) that narratology is a branch of poetics, and poetics is 'the systematic study of literature as literature' (p. 2); and 2) that the object of study in narratology is (or should be) the *differentia specifica* of narrative fiction (pp. 1–2).

Like poetics, narratology saw itself as a theory, conceived at the time as an attempt to formulate a system of logically interrelated laws, underlying the regularity of phenomena or of a group of phenomena. A theory was believed to be defined by its method(s), i.e., its research procedures, the questions it asks, the ways in which it accounts for the operation of the system. Method, in turn, determined the object of study, as distinct from the empirical object 'out there'. Poetics singled out 'literariness' or 'literature as literature' as its object of study, trying to define those characteristics that render a discourse specifically literary (e.g. Jakobson's 'poetic function', 1960). In a similar fashion, narratology also searched for *differentia specifica*, but – as I shall argue – it was less clear what these specific features characterized.

Under the aegis of structuralism and its formalist progenitors, the endeavour to construct a theory carried connotations of 'objectivity', 'neutrality', even 'scientificity' (Todorov, 1969; Hrushovski, 1976). The scientific aspirations resulted in a need to use a precise metalanguage, with a one-to-one relationship between term and phenomenon. Of the various branches of literary study, description seemed the one closest to the status of science, and indeed a description of the ways in which literature operates was conceived of as the goal of literary theory. But what was the goal, or object of study, of narratology? My introduction suggested that the goal was to define the *differentia specifica* of narrative fiction. Furthermore, a description of its features or properties was seen as a way of distinguishing it from non-narrative, non-verbal, and non-fictional discourses (1983, pp. 2–3).

But there was another direction in the discipline: one that sought the *differentia specifica* not of narrative fiction but of narrative in general, whether fictional or non-fictional, verbal or non-verbal. What this orientation wished to explore was often called 'narrativity' and was often claimed to reside in the 'story' abstracted from its manifestations in different media (see note 1 to my 1983 introduction, p. 133). Indeed, it was that orientation that was originally christened 'narratology', (Todorov 1969; Prince 1973), and I called mine 'poetics of narrative fiction' in order to emphasize the difference. Bal (1977, p. 13) spoke about two kinds of narratology general narratology, and 'literary narratology', to which she saw her own work as belonging. The first was (for Bal) a branch of textology (I myself would say 'semiotics'), the second, a sub-division of poetics. Since then, both kinds have come to be called 'narratology', and I now use the term accordingly even when reflecting on my own book. Nor is this merely a terminological matter. Various permutations and combinations of these two directions have become crucial in later developments of the discipline.

The underlying assumptions, as well as the definitions they generated, led narratology to exclude many aspects deemed by others to be central to the study of literature. Exclusions, one should remember, are the other side of a delimitation of a field. Many of these were a logical result of the limitation to 'story' ('general narratology'), but seemed less commensurate with 'a literary narratology'. Take, for example, my definition of 'narrative fiction' as 'the narration of a succession of fictional events' (p. 2). This implies 'the verbal nature of the medium' (p. 2) and thus excludes non-verbal narratives. The term 'narration', as some may have intuited even when reading the introduction, also emphasizes the narrator at the expense of the author, and indeed the first section of Chapter 7 validates this view. 'Fictional' obviously excludes non-fictional narratives, although not much is done in my book with what Cohn later called 'Signposts of Fictionality' (1999, pp. 109–131). The foregrounding of 'a succession of events' (p. 2) (there are slight differences in this respect among the formulations of different narratologists) gave rise to many interesting story-grammars (see Ch. 2) as well as to a sophisticated analysis of time (Genette 1972; Ch. 4 in my book), but it also subordinated character to action and did not develop any satisfactory theory of character (see Ch. 3). Under the influence of structuralism, narratology excluded theme, interpretation, the reader (Ch. 9 of my book, for example, subordinates the reader to the text), the referent(s), ideology, space, and even – as I argue in a later essay – language itself (1989, pp. 157–166).

NARRATOLOGY UNDER ATTACK

Both the underlying assumptions of narratology and the exclusions they entailed came under attack in the poststructuralist period. The attacks were also partly directed against narratology and partly against its structuralist basis, the distinction often being elusive. 'The systematic study of literature', with its aura of scientificity, has been questioned almost as frequently as it has been attempted, and I'll limit myself to a few examples. Evoking the Nietzschean uneasy but gay knowledge of the limitations of knowledge, Hillis-Miller undertook to disarticulate the notion of science (and/or show that it disarticulates itself) by pointing out contradictions and *aporias* which undermine the enterprise. He also challenged the 'schematizing rationality devoted to intellectual mastery', celebrating deconstruction – by contrast – as an 'expression' of the 'experience of the failure of an attempt at mastery' (e.g. 1980/81, p. 189). Furthermore, he claimed that the language of literature is dangerous to the scientific endeavour, inevitably 'contaminating' it with the illogical and the uncanny. In a similar vein, though with the additional dimension of Lacanian psychoanalysis, Felman's study of Henry James's *The Turn of the Screw* (1977, pp. 94–209) emphasized the position of mastery as a position of blindness, the determination to obtain knowledge as a kind of murder, and 'literature' as precisely that which escapes full knowledge and mastery. From a Bakhtinian perspective, Gary Saul Morson considered poetics (and narratology as one of its branches) as a limitation of contingency and process. Indeed, system seemed to him a way of mastering anxieties about process, his own agenda being the liberation of the latter by substituting 'tempics' for 'poetics' (1999, pp. 277–314).

It was not only 'the rage for order' (Henry James's expression) that was challenged. Other tenets of 'scientificity', e.g. objectivity and neutrality, also came under sceptical scrutiny, affecting the narratological dream of pure description in ways which I shall pursue shortly. Similarly, metalanguage was put in doubt by deconstruction and affiliated psychoanalytic approaches. The possibility of distinguishing between the language of literature and language *about* literature could no longer be taken for granted, and all language was said to be permeated by figurativity, indeterminacy, *aporias*. This, however, was not the only reason for the widespread dissatisfaction with the metalanguage of narratology. Most criticism had to do with the alienating effect of its specific 'jargon': its use of neologisms based on Greek roots, combined with the prefixes extra-, intra-, meta-, ana- or pro-. As Nünning amusingly puts it, 'To the utter bewilderment and dismay of generations of undergraduates, even narratological terms beginning with the prefixes hetero- and homo- did not have anything to do with sex [. . .]' (1999, p. 347). I'll have more to say about metalanguage later, but I now turn to the problematization of description.

Description, it has been argued in different quarters, is neither independent nor neutral, the two activities on which it depends most heavily being interpretation and ideology. Stanley Fish, for example, claims that 'formal units are always a function of the interpretive model one brings to bear (they are not "in the text")' (1980, p. 13). And indeed, even the labelling of events, with which a part of my second chapter is concerned, or the abstraction of the story from the text, are not free of interpretation. Different readers may arguably label events (or 'functions') differently, and may consequently abstract different (at least somewhat different) stories from the same text. Furthermore, just as description is now seen as interpretation-bound, both activities have been said to depend on ideology, whether overtly or covertly. By the same token, even 'neutrality' can be considered an ideological agenda, motivated by the desire to give narratology a scientific aura. It is often said that theory may gain by unmasking concealed ideologies, and theorists are often advised to 'position' themselves, to declare the perspective from which they write, rather than take shelter behind the appearance of objectivity and neutrality. Not only the 'purity' of description but also its position as the goal of narratology has been challenged. In 'The Point of Narratology', former narratologist Mieke Bal argues that narratological description should become a means rather than an end, its findings put to the service of cultural and ideological concerns, as well as to the study of non-narrative and non-verbal 'semiotic objects' (1990, p. 730).

A VARIETY OF NARRATOLOGICAL RESPONSES

Faced with scepticism concerning its presuppositions, as well as criticism of its exclusions, narratology reacted in several ways. While some theorists remained immune to the effects of destabilization, others (myself among them) could not ignore the impact of doubt. A relatively superficial symptom of this has been the infiltration of inverted commas whenever words such as 'fact', 'evidence', 'reality', 'truth', 'validity' are used. It seems to me today that the inverted commas may actually be a double symptom, signifying both the doubt and the desire to retain some aspect of the undermined notion. A more radical response is an attempt to incorporate deconstructive insights into narratology. O'Neill, for example, modifies previous narratological models so as to foreground his claim that 'narrative as a discursive system is always potentially subversive both of the story it ostensibly reconstructs and of its own telling of that story' (1994, p. 3). Other narratologists accepted the critique of pure description and proceeded to subordinate it to interpretation and ideology (e.g. Bal 1986, 1988, 1990, 1991; Lanser 1986), though doing so has sometimes resulted in accusations of 'betrayal' or a failure to understand on the part of purists (see Diengott 1988 against Lanser).

As to exclusions, there were quite a few attempts to integrate initially bracketed aspects into narratology. Space, for example, was (very partially) addressed under the category of 'description' relatively early in the development of the discipline (Hamon 1972; Bal 1977) and is now being re-thought from Bakhtinian and other perspectives. Theme became the subject of a collection of essays edited by Sollors in 1993 and a parallel volume published by Bremond, Landy and Pavel in 1995. The author was rethought, in different ways, by Chatman (1990), O'Neill (1994), Ginsburg and

Rimmon-Kenan (1999), and Darby (2001). The reader, in turn, became the centre of 'rhetorical narratology' (e.g. Phelan 1996, Rabinowitz 1997) and later of a special issue of *Narrative* devoted to 'Contemporary Narratology' (2001).

Not all exclusions, however, could be included without undermining the integrity of the discipline. New approaches developed, often having assumptions and agendas partly or fully adverse to narratology (and/or to structuralism): Reader Response Criticism (as distinct from the above-mentioned subordination of the reader to narratology), Ideological Critique, Feminism, New Historicism, Postcolonialism. Viewed in this way, the new approaches can be taken to supersede narratology (and certainly structuralism), and the implied story is about the rise and fall of the latter . . . Viewed differently, they (or some of their aspects) become new forms of narratology, and the 'rise and fall' is followed by 'the renaissance'. The 1983 conclusion of *Narrative Fiction* seems to me to oscillate between the two alternatives. It opens with the anxious question: 'Has this book been an introduction to or an obituary of the poetics of narrative fiction?' (p. 130) and then covers up the anxiety by the hopeful statement that 'the discipline is still alive and kicking, although (or perhaps because) it no longer enjoys the privilege of the latest fashion' (p. 130). From a perspective of time and a *penchant* for re-emergence, David Herman makes the following comment about that conclusion: 'Now, some fifteen years later, Rimmon-Kenan's cautious optimism concerning narratology appears to have been warranted. It seems in short that rumours of the death of narratology have been greatly exaggerated. Recently we have witnessed a small but unmistakable explosion of activity in narrative studies[. . .]' (1999, p. 1). Considering these developments a transformation, yet continuation of narratology, Herman suggests a convenient distinction between classical and postclassical narratology. On the basis of many more parameters than I have here disengaged from my 1983 introduction, Herman compares the classical and postclassical stances, his sympathies being clearly with the latter. In good 'classical' fashion, though not without reservations about schematization, Ansgar Nünning systematizes the differences in the form of binary oppositions. With his permission, I reproduce his table here:

structuralist ('classical') narratology	cultural and historical narratology, and other new ('postclassical') narratologies
text-centered	context-oriented
main focus on closed systems and static products	main focus on open and dynamic processes
'features', 'properties' of a text as a main object of study	the dynamics of the reading process (reading strategies, interpretive choices, preference rules)
bottom-up analyses	top-down syntheses
preference for (reductive) binarisms and graded scales	preference for holistic cultural interpretation and 'thick descriptions'
emphasis on theory, formalist description, and taxonomy of narrative techniques	emphasis on application, thematic readings, and ideologically-charged evaluations
evasion of moral issues and the production of meaning	focus on ethical issues and the dialogic negotiation of meanings
establishing a grammar of narrative and a poetics of fiction as main goals	putting the analytic toolbox to interpretative use as main goals
formalist and descriptivist paradigm	interpretative and evaluative paradigm
ahistorical and synchronous in orientation	historical and diachronous in orientation
focus on universalist features of all narratives	focus on particular effects of individual narratives
a unified (sub)discipline	an interdisciplinary project

(Nünning 1999, p. 358).

POSTCLASSICAL NARRATOLOGIES

The shift from a fairly unified discipline to one characterised by a diversity of approaches is emphasized by the felicitous use of the plural in Herman's title: *Narratologies*. Beyond the diversity the discipline also opens up to interdisciplinarity. Both types of branching-out are evident in current labels such as 'contextualist narratology', 'marxist narratology', 'feminist narratology', 'postcolonial narratology', 'cognitive narratology', ' "natural" narratology', 'postmodern narratology', 'possible worlds theory' (see, e.g. Nünning 1999, pp. 351–52).

The plethora of new narratological approaches is indeed remarkable. Even more striking, I think, as well as moving, is Nünning's comment on the recurrence of the preposition 'towards' in the titles of many studies proposing a transition from classical narratology to some variety of the postclassical: 'It is a consoling thought, however, that there are many people on the move towards some end or other. In fact, narratologists always seem to be moving towards new destinations, but apparently they hardly ever get there, as is shown by the impressive number of titles of books and articles beginning with "towards".' (1999, p. 356). I consider this an insightful description of the state of the art. I also find it moving, because it corresponds to my sense of my own work since the days of 'classical narratology'. After a period of near-paralysis, caused by the destabilization of my 'certain certainties', I tried to move – not 'towards', but tentatively 'beyond'. *A Glance Beyond Doubt* (1996) was an attempt to reinstate representation and rehumanize subjectivity, integrating the contemporary problematization of these concepts and going beyond it. It was also an attempt to theorize through literature, to use novels as, in some sense, the source of theory. At the same time, I embarked upon research in a few interdisciplinary junctions – literature and psychoanalysis (see e.g. 1987), historiography, legal studies. The same change is evidenced in the relation between my teaching and my writing. Whereas *Narrative Fiction* was based on courses entitled 'Introduction to Narrative Fiction' or 'Poetics of Narrative', I now teach seminars called 'Narrative Theory Reconsidered' and 'The Concept of Narrative in Different Disciplines'. As in Nünning's description, I feel like many of those people 'on the move', in a state of an exciting perpetual 'towards', never quite making it to a destination. It is from this perspective that I wish to devote the rest of this chapter to the condition of 'towards'.

TOWARDS: A VARIETY OF POSSIBILITIES

'Towards' as paralysing oscillation

'Towards' is usually associated with an intermediary stage, place, or position, 'in the direction of', 'in the area or vicinity of', 'turned to, facing'. When it becomes an apparent permanent condition, as Nünning's statement suggests, 'towards' tends to border on 'between', and this may be a possible indication of a deadlock. I shall argue that there may be a much more appealing potential in 'towards'. In the meantime, however, I wish to suggest that the delicate balance (or less delicate tension?) between what Piaget long ago called 'transform-ation' and 'self-regulation' in the relations between 'classical' and 'postclassical' narratologies may have caused a certain mutual neutral-ization or stasis. One aspect of these relations needs to be emphasized in order to lend plausibility to the foregoing suggestion. It stands to reason that not all feminism, marxism, new historicism, psycho-analysis, or postcolonialism are narratological, nor would they conceive of themselves in this way.

Nevertheless, there is an area of overlap in which new approaches ask narratological questions or use narratological methods and analytic categories, often in subordination to their own purposes. If, for example, a study of gender utilizes the notion of 'voice', accompanied by some typology of narrators and/or focalizers (as Lanser 1986 does), or if 'textuality' is added to the three basic aspects of narrative fiction (Rimmon-Kenan 1983, p. 3) in order to account for the ways narratives potentially subvert themselves (O'Neill 1994), the appellations 'femi-nist narratology' and 'postmodern narratology' seem to me justified. In some sense, then, it is precisely those forms of the new approaches that *can* be seen as narratological that are Janus-faced: one face turning in the direction of 'the new', be it feminism, new historicism, or postcolonialism, the other in the direction of classical narratology. Thus, it may be precisely those features of the new approaches which make sense of their alliance with narratology that simultaneously prevent them from fully reaching their feminist, new historicist or postcolonial destinations; this being an inevitable result of their condition as 'overlap' (*differentia specifica* at the back door, I realize – if not of the object of study, at least of the discipline).

'Towards' as mutual modification

Pulling in two directions, however, is not the only possible relation between classical and postclassical narratologies. Many theorists (myself included) attempt a negotiation between the different orientations, involving mutual modification, partial combinations, and shifts of emphasis. Thus quite a few specific 'classical' narratological categories have undergone re-thinking and the apparatus as a whole now tends to be seen not as 'features' or 'properties' of narrative texts, but as implied reading potentials informing the interaction between reader and text, between interpretive communities and texts, between a culture's encoded ideology and a reader's compliant or resistant decoding. In spite of criticism and changes, however, numerous postclassical studies pay tribute to 'the usefulness of narratology' (e.g. Bal 1990, p. 729. See also Lanser 1986, p. 346) or its importance as an 'analytical toolkit' (e.g. Nünning 1999, p. 348). Narratology, even of the classical brand, still 'works', I believe, for historical and anthropological reasons: cultures consciously or unconsciously generate narrative structures, patterns, processes as one mode of perceiving, constructing, making sense of things and experiences. Narratology, in turn, gives names and a relational network to them. As long as narratives permeate cultures, narratology (in whatever modified form) is likely to remain effective. Moreover, narratology is also helpful in identifying and characterizing 'deviations' from and subversions of its purported system. Exceptions can only be discerned against the background of the rule, and narratology formulates some of the regularities which specific narratives gloriously defy.

Without discounting the instrumentality of the analytical categories suggested by narratology, the 'toolkit approach' strikes me as insufficient. I would still want to claim the status of theory for narratology, but my conception of 'theory' is influenced by postclassical interrogations. Indeed, it is difficult today to attribute objectivity, neutrality, scientificity to narratology (or to 'the sciences' themselves). My present understanding of 'theory', therefore, is somewhat attenuated. I would now see it as a self-conscious reflection, a conceptual framework, a set of hypotheses having explanatory power. Theory, in this sense, is valuable both in itself and as something that enables a set of analytic procedures which is still generally said to 'work'. As to metalanguage, the terminology developed by classical narratology may have been too arcane, but this − I think − is not a sufficient reason for dismissing any attempt to establish consensual working definitions of phenomena. 'Call it Ivan Ivanowitz', Roman Jakobson once said, 'as long as I know what you are talking about'.

On the one hand, the interaction with postclassical narratologies makes me limit the conditions required by the notion of 'theory'; on the other, it invites a broadening of the theory's object of study. From today's perspective, I would drop the word 'fiction' from the title of this book, as well as the term 'poetics' from its sub-title. The epistemological question of fictionality receives very little attention in my study (as I have already remarked), and the subordination to poetics spells out what was implied by the misleading term 'fiction', i.e., that the book was meant as a contribution to 'literary narratology' (Bal 1977). Today, I am more concerned with 'narrativity' than with 'literary narratology'. However, unlike the story-oriented researchers mentioned earlier, my interest is not predominantly in grammars of an abstracted succession of events, but in the variety of ways in which these are shaped, formed, in different media and different types of discourse. This combination of partial aspects of what used to be alternative directions in narratology characterizes one difference between my past and present preoccupations, explaining my turn to interdisciplinarity from a perspective that remains narratological.

In many interdisciplinary junctions (e.g. literature and psychoanalysis, philosophy, historiography, legal studies), the very concept of narrative has been broadened, partly under the influence of constructivist theories in the social sciences, to designate a manner of perceiving, organizing, constructing meaning, a mode of cognition different from − but in no way inferior to − logical or discursive thinking. Hence Brooke-Rose's sequel to the question with which I started this chapter: 'Whatever happened to narratology? It *got swallowed into story* seems the obvious answer' (1991, p. 16). I interpret 'swallowed into' not only as a description but also as a warning note (although Brooke-Rose did not necessarily mean it this way). On the one hand, it is precisely the success of narratology that can be gleaned from the sweeping generalization of its main concepts. On the other hand, the generalizing tendency runs the risk of obliterating narratology's object of study. If any discourse is a narrative (as fashion would often have it nowadays), the term may be emptied of all semantic content. Classical narratology, it seems to me, can contribute to highlighting the principles underlying all narratives (not only literary ones).

A case in point is a recent essay by David Darby, arguing that my 1983 'redefinition of the implied author as a depersonified "construct inferred and assembled by the reader . . . a set of implicit norms"' opens up to 'the larger cultural discourses that have come to represent the concerns of contemporary narratology' (2001, pp. 838–839). In his opinion, my notion has the potential of becoming 'the point of intersection between formal rhetoric and context' (p. 846), anticipating future developments. My attitude to the author (whether implied or not) has in the meantime undergone modifications (Cf. Ginsburg and Rimmon-Kenan 1999), and I am not sure that this is the concept I would use as a point of intersection. However, the idea that classical narratological categories may contain a postclassical potential strikes me as insightful. From my present interdisciplinary perspective, I would single out two such concepts: 'narration' and 'dual temporality'.

Narration is in no way restricted to literature. In order to make sense of experiences, people consciously or unconsciously, audibly or inaudibly, tell stories to themselves as well as to others. Narratives are governed by a dual time-scheme owing to the ontological gap between the succession of signs and the temporality of events (in whatever expanded definition). I am aware, of course, of the postmodern questioning of such a metaphysical assumption, but it seems to me that even after collapsing hierarchy and primacy, there remains at least a difference in manifestation between what are perhaps only aspects of the same signifying chain. At any rate, the postclassical potential of classical narratological categories is one more form of 'towards' as mutual negotiation.

'Towards' as perpetual change

In the foregoing pages, I have tried to show that 'towards' need not be confined to a paralysing oscillation between classical and post-classical narratologies but may also connote a mutual modification, potentially evolving a composite theory. Moreover, 'towards' may suggest yet another, more radical, meaning. While it habitually functions as a preposition, the dictionary also lists a rare usage as an adjective, meaning 'in progress'. In this sense, 'towards' need not indicate a movement from one place, position, stage, to another, but may rather evoke an intransitive process.[2] Eschewing finalization, such a conception valorizes, rather than deplores, not arriving at a destination. From this vantage point, narratology is not a 'once-and-for-all', closed theory but a mode of theorizing that is open, dynamic, neverending.

Under the influence of Bakhtin (1981, 1984) and that of the philosopher of science Mara Beller (2001), I have been pondering such a possibility for quite some time, but have not yet developed it fully (i.e., it is itself in a condition of 'towards'). Moreover, a fully-fledged development of this mode of thinking would go beyond narratology to literary theory at large, as well as beyond *literary* theory. Let me therefore make a few preliminary comments, revolving around the notion of 'towards'. Although I consider these reflections a new phase in my thinking, I would not be surprised if some readers saw them as yet another variation on the spiralling movement with which I ended my 1983 conclusion. Indeed, twenty years from now (if I live that long) I myself may say that in retrospect the present ending also covers up an anxiety. But here goes: Perhaps instead of experiencing classical and postclassical narratologies as neutralizing each other (possibility 1 above), or trying to make them conform to each other in a negotiation that makes each modify aspects of itself in the light of the other (possibility 2 above), the approach I am groping towards would emphasize precisely the *differences* between them. In the spirit of the narratological quest for the basic unit of 'story', the dialogical approach might claim that the basic unit of theorizing is disagreement, fruitful disagreement, leading to continuous change. Referring to science, Beller says:

Disagreement can lead to novelty, rather than to merely futile controversy, only if there is a basic open-mindedness, lack of dogmatism, element of ignorance, uncertainty, and genuine doubt at the frontier of science. The existence of doubt (disagreement with oneself), as well as disagreement with others, is a necessary condition for the occurrence of scientific change.

(2001, p. 12 typescript)

I wish to suggest that similar characteristics can make narratology an ever-changing, open-ended creative process – indeed, a perpetual 'towards'.

NOTES

1 INTRODUCTION

1 In this sense, my object of study is at once broader and narrower than what is often called 'narratology'. It is broader in that it treats more aspects of narrative fiction than those which are transferable from one medium to another. It is narrower in that it treats those transferable aspects only in relation to their manifestation in literature, not in other media. Of course, not all theorists restrict 'narratology' to the transferable aspect of narrative (as do Todorov 1969 and Prince 1973). Some use the term to designate a study of all aspects of narrative. Bal (1977, p.21) for example, claims that narration (plus perspective) is the narratological problem *par excellence* (on p.13 she explicitly talks about two kinds of narratology).

2 This distinction recalls cognate mappings of the field, like the Formalists' *'fabula'* v. *'sjužet'* (e.g. Tomashevsky 1965, p. 66), Todorov's *'histoire'* v. *'discours'* (1966, p. 126), Chatman's 'story' v. 'discourse' (1978, p. 19), Barthes's *'fonctions'*, *'actions'*, *'narration'* (1966, p. 6), and Bal's *'histoire'*, *'récit'*, *'texte narratif'* (1977, pp. 4–8). Unfortunately, since many readers of this book may not be familiar with the other classifications, I refrain from comparing them with mine.

3 The description of story and narration as metonymies of the text is inspired by Perry (1979, p.43) who discusses in this way the relations between the text and the implied reader.

2 STORY: EVENTS

1 This chapter relies heavily on a draft prepared by Moshe Ron; quite a few passages are copied verbatim from that draft. However, the general conception, the substance, the order of the items, and the style have undergone serious changes, so that (unfortunately for me) Ron can no longer be held responsible for the weaknesses of the chapter.

2 A classical structuralist move. See Hjelmslev 1961, pp. 47–60; Barthes 1970, pp. 39–41. Orig. publ. in French 1964; Greimas 1966, pp. 25–7.

3 See also Barthes 1966, p. 1; Todorov 1966, pp. 126–7; Pavel 1973b, p. 1. Others presuppose some version of this claim by treating models evolved for one semiotic and cultural domain as unproblematically transferable to another domain. Note that my own study speaks of 'aspects' rather than 'levels'.

4 An argument diagnosing translatability as a presupposition of metaphysical discourse will be found in Derrida 1977. Orig. publ. in French 1972.

5 The clearest and most explicit account of such considerations is in Pavel, unpublished typescript; also in Pavel 1973a, 1973b, 1976. In recent years Pavel has been developing a highly promising model under the name of 'move grammar', a preliminary version of which can be found in 1978. In this model Pavel borrows the tree-like presentation used in transformational grammar.

6 See, however, Greimas 1970, p. 187; Hénault 1979, p. 122, and Groupe d'Entrevernes 1979, p.137 for ways of dynamizing the square with the help of which Greimas represents the deep structure (on the square see pp. 12–13).

7 Like Greimas, I shall also treat Propp's theory under the heading of 'surface structure', although it clearly antedates the transformational-generative model in linguistics.

8 As the term implies, a 'mytheme' (coined on 'phoneme', 'morpheme' etc.) is the minimal unit of myth.

9 Greimas uses the term *'énoncé narratif'*, confusingly rendered into English in the 1977 translation as 'narrative utterance'.

10 The determination of the basic story-unit is a point much in debate. One term often used to designate such a unit is 'function'. However, since this term involves a specific view of story, I prefer to begin with the more neutral 'event' and shall introduce the notion of function in a later section, pp. 20–2.

11 One way of circumventing this problem would be to speak, as Prince

does (1973), of 'stative' and 'active' events, but this seems an artificial terminological solution.

12 Note that there is no distinction here between the text and the story or plot abstracted from it, with the consequence that story and plot are contrasted as mutually exclusive narrative forms. If I use 'plot' at all – and I am rather wary of a term which has become too vague in ordinary critical usage – I take it to designate one type of story (the type which emphasizes causality) rather than a narrative form opposed to the story.

13 By the way, it is evident that a manipulation of the paraphrase may transform many single events into minimal stories of this sort (e.g. The king died → The king was alive and well, then he drank some poison, then, as a result he was dead and buried). This goes back to my point on pp. 15–16.

14 The final paragraph of the *text* (not necessarily evidence for the structure of the *story*) is clearly meant to forestall any sense of closure: 'And it seemed to them that in only a few more minutes a solution would be found and a new, beautiful life would begin; but both of them knew very well that the end was still a long, long way away and that the most complicated and difficult part was only just beginning' (1927, p. 26. Orig. publ. in Russian 1899).

15 Note that these are strikingly similar to Prince's 'minimal story' (p. 18).

16 However, as this freedom applies both to the composition *of* the story and to participants *in* the story, there often results confusion between the two types of causal and teleological links distinguished above (pp. 17–18): the intent or volition of a character may be mistaken for a structural principle of the plot. In order to avoid this confusion, Ron's Oedipus chart tags the sequences with the name of the character whose long-term interests (though not necessarily conscious will or knowledge) are at stake. That Bremond's method cannot consistently represent the possible discrepancy between the participants' intent and the narrative relevance of their actions is, I believe, a serious flaw. Characters often do not realize what they are doing. Thus Oedipus' intent and his attempt to ward off the dangers of which he learned from the oracle at Delphi do not have the same status as his failure to do so (this is true of all the sequences ending in failure on the charts), whereas in the sequence pitting Oedipus against the sphinx (Chart II) all three stages are within his awareness and consistent with his role as agent.

3 STORY: CHARACTERS

1 (a) 'Allotropy' means 'variation of physical properties without change of substance' *(OED)*. (b) For other statements about the obliteration of individuality by a sense of uniformity see Mauriac in Roudiez 1961/2, p. 553 and McCarthy 1961, p. 176.

2 There is a clear interaction between the 'anti-novel' and the structuralist 'school' in France (see, for example, Barthes on Robbe-Grillet, 1964).

3 As is well known, this tendency was attacked by Knights in 'How many children had Lady Macbeth?' (1964. Orig. publ. 1933).

4 Although Hamon takes a sentence for convenience, one should remember that Greimas is concerned with narrative (or semiotic) categories, and these are not identical with linguistic ones.

5 (a) It should be remembered that even in 1970 Barthes sees character as a network of textual signs, not as a full being, and that even in the same book there are different statements about the same subject, but it is still interesting that the subordination to action is no longer categorically maintained. (b) For an interesting discussion of how a function becomes a proper name and how the proper name becomes a character, see Kermode 1979, pp. 75–99.

6 It is possible for a character to be concentrated in one textual segment, but this is fairly unusual (Hrushovski, forthcoming).

7 Bartohes's own term, *'sème'*, is much less anthropomorphic. In fact, Chatman explicitly models his theory of character on psychological theories of personality, whereas Barthes considers character a textual junction.

8 I am grateful to Professor Hrushovski for stimulating discussions on which the following presentation (pp. 37–8) is based. However, since the selection, synthesis, and examples are mine he should in no way be held responsible for the weaknesses of the presentation. What will be introduced below is only a part of Hrushovski's theory of character which is itself a part of his unified theory of the text (both forthcoming). An outline of the general theory can be found in Hrushovski 1974, 1976a, 1979.

9 In this connection, see Chatman's own statement which ignores the directional dimension: 'Events travel as vectors, "horizontally" from earlier to later. Traits, on the other hand, extend over time-spans staked out by the events' (1978, p. 129). Hrushovski's theory, on the other hand, is able to account for the directionality ignored by Chatman. On directionality see also Even-Zohar 1968/9, pp. 538–68.

10 This point was made by Professor Baruch Hochman in a personal conversation.
11 Forster himself implicitly recognizes this possibility when he speaks of 'the beginning of the curve toward the round' (1963, p. 75).
12 I owe this point to Professor H. M. Daleski.
13 This third axis, suggested by Ewen in 1971, is replaced in 1980 by the 'mimetic and symbolic axis'. Since the latter seems to me of a different order from the first two, I retain the original classification.

4 TEXT: TIME

1 The foregoing general considerations are based on Moshe Ron's lecture notes.
2 One should note, however, two factors which tone down the irreversibility of text-time: (a) the fact of writing and hence the possibility of re-reading; (b) the existence of quasi-spatial patterns which establish supra-linear links, e.g. analogy.
3 Since I follow Genette rather closely, I shall not give page references for every point taken from him; instead, I prefer to acknowledge here a debt greater than footnotes can express. See also Rimmon 1976a, pp. 33–62, from which I often quote verbatim without page reference, considering self-plagiarism a legitimate activity.
4 I 'rewrite' his *'histoire'* and *'récit'* as 'story' and 'text' in order to preserve the consistency of my own terminology throughout the presentation.
5 More about gaps in chapter 9.
6 Genette in fact says that prolepsis is incompatible with suspense (1972, p. 105). The above formulation is my modification.
7 The traditional typology of narrators will be modified in chapter 7 with the help of Genette's different categories.
8 As Genette says, this was already proposed by Günther Müller in 1948.
9 It should be noted at this point that additional difficulties often emerge when story-duration is neither discussed nor inferable.
10 Not every pause is descriptive, and not every description is a pause (Genette 1972, pp. 128–9).
11 In a footnote (1972, p. 146) Genette says that his typology of frequencies does not include another possibility for which he knows no example, namely that of narrating several times an event which 'happened' several times but a different number of times. There is an interesting example of this type in Faulkner's 'A Rose for Emily'

(1930). The text narrates four times an event which is said to have happened every Sunday for a period of about two years – Emily's and Baron's defiant ride in a yellow-wheeled buggy. This was pointed out to me by a graduate student, Anat Epstein.

5 TEXT: CHARACTERIZATION

1 (a) A great deal of what is said in this chapter derives from Ewen 1971, 1980, with modifications and examples of my own. (b) Ewen speaks of direct and indirect means of characterization. I have, however, changed his labels, since his first category includes only one mean(s).

2 However, there are texts, like Lawrence's *Sons and Lovers* (1913), where such definitions clash with indirect characterizations, and the result is perplexing.

3 This is a modified version of a classification proposed by H. M. Daleski in his lectures of 1965. Daleski includes 'act of the mind' and 'symbolic act' in the same classification. However, these seem to me to be based on different criteria and will therefore be integrated into other parts of this chapter.

4 The 'natural' causality is: X is brave, therefore he killed the dragon; Y is a snob, therefore she uses many foreign words.

5 In 1971 Ewen treats 'analogous characterization' on a par with direct and indirect characterization. In 1980 he seems to hesitate between subordinating it to indirect presentation (p. 48) and treating it as an independent type of characterization (pp. 99–100) in spite of an insight into its different status (pp. 100–1) on which my comment above is based.

6 TEXT: FOCALIZATION

1 Genette also links 'focalization' to the term proposed by Brooks and Warren (1959. Orig. publ. 1943): 'focus of narration'.

2 I have grave doubts about the validity of the personification of narrative agents (i.e. treating them as if they were people). Indeed, this is why I use the term 'agent'. Nevertheless, there is a touch of personification at this point of the discussion – retained because it may be one of the causes of the confusion which I am trying to explain.

3 Although in the book as a whole Booth talks about 'point of view' and narration as if they were the same phenomenon, he does not confuse the two in his discussion of Stephen (1961, p. 163).

4 The terminology pertaining to narration will be modified in chapter 7.

5 The situation is, in fact, more complex, since the narrator Pip also often acts as focalizer, and the story is sometimes focalized by the experiencing child and sometimes by the adult narrator.

6 My distinction between external and internal focalization deliberately departs from Genette's classification of *récits* into non-focalized, internally focalized and externally focalized (1972, pp. 206–7). His 'non-focalized' corresponds to my 'external focalization' and his 'internally focalized' is analogous to my 'internal focalization'. His third category ('externally focalized'), however, is based on a different criterion and will be integrated elsewhere in my discussion. As Bal has convincingly argued (1977, pp. 28–9), Genette's classification is based on two different criteria: while the distinction between non-focalized and internally focalized refers to the position of the perceiver (the focalizer), that between internally focalized and externally focalized refers to the perceived object (the focalized). Stanzel's use of 'external' and 'internal' (1981, pp. 5–6) seems to be close to mine, as is Uspeusky's (1973, p. 130 and elsewhere).

7 This distinction can be profitably related to the axis of 'penetration into the inner life', discussed in the chapter on character (pp. 41–2).

8 The following discussion is based mainly on Uspensky (1973. Orig. publ. in Russian 1970), with my own modifications, but also on similar categories suggested by Chatman (1978), Stanzel (1981) and Ron (unpublished). Uspensky does not always distinguish between narration and focalization, nor does he distinguish between the narrator and the author.

9 Uspensky does not use the term 'panoramic', which I borrow from Lubbock 1963. Orig. publ. 1921.

10 These terms should be taken metaphorically when applied to a narrative agent rather than to a living person.

11 Uspensky gives this example under the rubric 'subjective/objective'. However, it seems to me that subjectivity and objectivity belong to the emotive component more than to the cognitive one, and the passages from *The Idiot*, on the other hand, exemplify cognitive rather than emotive focalization. Uspensky does not distinguish between these two types, treating both together under 'psychological'.

12 (a) Uspensky also shows a similar handling of Russian v. French speech in *War and Peace*. (b) Uspensky treats such verbal indicators as a 'phraseological plane', on a par with the other facets (or 'planes', in his terminology) of focalization (or 'point of view', in his language). As

should be clear from my own presentation, I see phraseology as a way of conveying focalization, not as one of its facets. I also avoid the term 'plane' because it seems to me to suggest a misleadingly hierarchical conception.

13 I am grateful to Ruth Ginsburg for working on this text with me.

7 NARRATION: LEVELS AND VOICES

1 Gibson (1950) talks about the 'mock reader'.

2 It is also difficult to see how 'it' – a non-personal implied entity – can be said to have 'chosen' the means of communication (Chatman 1978, p. 148).

3 See the debate between Bal and Bronzwaer (1 981, pp.193–2 10).

4 Such statements undermine Chatman's caution when explaining that his category of 'non-narrated stories' could be called 'minimally nar-rated' (e.g. p. 147). The impression one gets is that in spite of his desire to forestall potential objections, Chatman does believe in non-narrated stories (see also p. 155 about a passage from Joyce's *Ulysses:* 'There *is* no narrator').

5 Fowler (1977, p. 78) expresses a similar view in agreeing with Booth. Chatman's view, on the other hand, appears to be influenced by the linguists Kuroda (1973, 1975) and Banfield (1973, 1978a, 1978b, 1981) who in turn are close, on this issue, to the German scholar Kate Ham-burger (1973. Orig. publ. in German 1957).

6 If one accepts Derrida's view *of 'différance'* (1973) no narration can ever be simultaneous with the action. What is conventionally accepted as 'simultaneous narration' is then a narration which is minimally distanced from the action.

7 My discussion of narrative levels relies heavily on Genette's (1972, pp. 238–51), but the examples are mostly mine. I prefer Bal's 'hypodi-egetic' (1977, pp. 24, 59–85) to Genette's 'metadiegetic', because the latter is confusing in view of the opposed meaning of 'meta' in logic and linguistics (a level above, not below). Genette apologizes for this confusion on p. 239 n. 1. See further discussion in Bal, 1981, pp. 41–59.

8 This text is mentioned in the New Accents series by both Rawkes (1977) and Fowler (1977) for various experimental techniques. For a detailed discussion of this novel see Rimmon-Kenan 1982.

9 These are Chatman's terms (1978, pp. 197–252). However, I include his 'non-narrated stories' under the category of covert narration.

Booth describes the same phenomena as 'dramatized' v. 'undramatized' narrators (1961, pp. 151–3).

10 Note that 'on this side' may indicate a combination of the narrator's reporting with a focalizer's perception. See chapters 6 and 8 (the section on FID).

11 For a different approach to unreliability, considering it not a feature of narrators but an aspect of the reader's organizing activity and extending the notion to the whole fictional world, see Yacobi 1981, pp. 113–26.

8 NARRATION: SPEECH REPRESENTATION

1 This imitative capacity of literature has not always gone unchallenged, and is strongly contested by deconstructionists today.

2 Genette treats the whole issue of diegesis v. mimesis under the heading of 'mode'. Contrary to Genette, I believe that these are two ways of narrating, not two ways of perceiving, perceptions becoming here one of the objects of the narration.

3 Free indirect discourse will henceforth be abridged as FID, direct discourse as DD and indirect discourse as ID.

4 Although the study of this phenomenon received a special impetus in the last ten years, there are earlier descriptions which should be mentioned. In Germany and Switzerland the phenomenon was called 'erlebte Rede' and investigated by such people as Bühler 1936; Glauser 1948; Hamburger 1951; Meyer 1957; Spitozer 1928 (and see the instructive synthesis in Hebrew by Joseph Ewen 1968, pp. 140–58; English abstract pp. xii–xiii). In France it was called 'style indirect libre' and studied mainly by Bally (1912) and Lips (1926). Ullmann (1957) was the first to introduce the term 'free indirect style' into English criticism. In Israel the phenomenon was variously discussed as 'combined speech' (Golomb 1968), 'represented speech' (Ewen 1968) and 'combined discourse' (Perry forthcoming).

5 What follows relies heavily on McHale 1978, pp. 251–2. As opposed to the traditional grammatical view which derives ID from DD and FID from ID, Banfield (1973) demonstrates the implausibility of such derivation. Like McHale (1978, p. 257), I retain the seemingly derivational description as a convenience in exposition. McHale also lists various indices which make readers recognize FID, and these are not only grammatical.

6 As McHale points out, Bakhtin and Voloshinov were not interested in the linguistic distinctions among types of discourse but in translin-

guistic distinctions 'based on the kinds and degrees of dialogic rela-
tionships holding between different utterances in a text, or between
utterances in different texts' (1978, p. 263).

9 THE TEXT AND ITS READING

1   To mention only the most prominent representatives of this orienta-
    tion: Riffaterre (1966), Fish (1970, 1980), Prince (1973) and Culler
    (1975) in America; Barthes (1970) in France; Iser (1971a, 1971b, 1974,
    1978), Warning (1975) and Jauss (1977) in Germany; (1979) in Italy;
    Hrushovski (1974, 1976a), Sternberg (1974a, 1974b, 1976) and Perry
    (1968a, 1969, 1974, 1976, 1979 and – with Sternberg – 1968b) in Israel.
       For reviews of works by Eco, Ingarden, Iser, and Jauss see Dolezel
    (1980, pp. 181–8), Brinker (1980, pp. 203–12) and Barnouw (1980,
    pp. 213–22) respectively. I would like to mention in this connection an
    MA thesis by Ruth Ginsburg which has helped me organize some of
    my thoughts on the subject. The thesis is entitled 'The Impossible
    Task of the Reader: A Reading of Kafka's Texts' (The Hebrew University
    of Jerusalem, 1980. In Hebrew).
2   For grammatical convenience I shall continue saying 'he', in spite of
    the foregoing explanation.
3   Similar comments on the dynamics of reading, though sometimes
    couched in different terms, can be found in Iser 1971a, pp. 283, 287;
    Eco 1979, p. 32; Brinker 1980, p. 206. In order to avoid a terminological
    confusion I have chosen to adhere to one presentation, and Perry's
    seemed the most exhaustive.
4   The foregoing paragraph is based on Moshe Ron's lecture notes.
5   According to Culler, 'naturalization' is often used in structuralist poet-
    ics as interchangeable with 'recuperation', 'motivation' and 'vrais-
    emblablisation'. Nevertheless, he points out subtle differences among
    them (1975, pp. 137–3), and there are others which he does not
    mention.
       While the three other terms originated in French Structuralism,
    'motivation' derives from Russian Formalism, although it is also used
    (often with a different emphasis) in Structuralism (see Sternberg
    (forthcoming) for the difference between Genette's use and that of the
    Formalists, as well as for differences among the Formalists them-
    selves). 'Motivation' is also used by the Tel-Aviv school, and I would
    have been tempted to equate it with 'naturalization' for the sake of an
    elegant synthesis. However, as Sternberg points out (forthcoming),

'motivation' is based on means-ends relations while 'naturalization' concerns forms and conditions of intelligibility and integration. Moreover, 'motivation' is author-oriented, while 'naturalization' is reader-oriented. These may be differences in methodological emphasis (ibid.), but they may also be basic ideological differences, and since this chapter is more reader-oriented than author-oriented, I have decided to avoid confusion and cling to 'naturalization'. Where the two notions can be conveniently related, I shall point this out. Part of the problem may be solved if one follows Perry in seeing both author and reader as metonymies of the text.

6 Sternberg (forthcoming), who speaks about 'motivation' rather than 'naturalization', calls the two principles 'quasi-mimetic or referential' v. 'aesthetic or rhetorical'. Perry (1979, pp. 36–42) talks about 'model oriented motivations' v. 'rhetorical or reader-oriented motivations'. I would like to emphasize that both types are based on *models*, and would also like to eschew the problem of the mimetic, quasi-mimetic, or referential status of reality in fiction. My own terms will therefore be 'reality model(s)' (i.e. the motivation or naturalization is not based on reality itself but on a model the human mind constructs to be able to conceive of it) v. 'literature model(s)'. The original, Formalist distinction was tripartite: realistic, compositional and artistic motivation (Tomashevsky 1965. Orig. publ. in Russian 1925). However, Sternberg has rightly argued (forthcoming) that the 'compositional' is actually a subtype of the 'artistic'.

7 In the specific context, this is a misleading interpretation, since Zambinella is a *castrato*. The text misleads the reader on purpose by appealing to his reality models.

11 TOWARDS . . .

1 Darby (2001, pp. 829–852) gives an account of the history of narratology which includes what he calls the French and North American structuralist tradition, the German formalist approach, and the Tel Aviv functionalist school.

2 I use 'intransitive' in the quasi-metaphoric sense in which Barthes calls 'to write' an 'intransitive verb', 1970, pp. 134–45.

REFERENCES

The items listed here are presented in two series: (1) works of narrative fiction and (2) theoretical studies. The first series consists of those narrative works which are either quoted or discussed in some detail, but does not include works which are merely mentioned in passing. The second series includes all the theoretical studies mentioned, quoted or analysed, so as to represent as many as possible of the texts which have influenced my thinking on this subject. Consequently, the second series is quite extensive (though not exhaustive), including many items which would appear in other *New Accents* books in a 'Further Reading' section. Those works which are most important for this study are annotated and marked with an asterisk.

WORKS OF NARRATIVE FICTION

Beckett, Samuel (1972) *Watt.* London: Calder & Boyars. Orig. publ. in French 1953.

Bellow, Saul (1973) *Herzog.* Harmondsworth: Penguin. Orig. publ. 1964.

Bierce, Ambrose (1952) 'Oil of Dog', in *The Collected Writings of Ambrose Bierce.* New York: Citadel Press. Orig. publ. in Bierce's *The Parenticide Club*, 1909–12.

Borges, Jorge Luis (1974) 'The Garden of Forking Paths' and 'Pierre Menard, Author of the Quixote', in *Labyrinths.* Harmondsworth: Penguin. Orig. publ. in Spanish 1956.

Brooke-Rose, Christine (1975) *Thru*. London: Hamish Hamilton.

Butor, Michel (1957) *La Modification*. Paris: Minuit.

Cervantes, Miguel de (1950) *Don Quixote*. Harmondsworth: Penguin. Orig. publ. in Spanish 1605–16.

Chaucer, Geoffrey (1934) *The Canterbury Tales*. Garden City, NY: Garden City Books. Orig. publ. 1390-1400 approx.

Chekhov, Anton (1927) 'Sleepy', in *Selected Tales of Tchehov*. London: Chatto & Windus. Orig. publ. in Russian 1888.

—— (1927) 'Lady with a Lapdog', in *Selected Tales of Tchehov*. London: Chatto & Windus. Orig. publ. in Russian 1899.

Conrad, Joseph (1975) *Heart of Darkness*. Harmondsworth: Penguin. Orig. publ. 1902.

—— (1963) *Nostromo*. Harmondsworth: Penguin. Orig. publ. 1904.

Cortázar, Julio (1967) *Hopscotch*. New York: Signet. Orig. publ. in Spanish 1963.

Dickens, Charles (1964) *Bleak House*. New York: Signet. Orig. publ. 1853.

—— (1978) *Great Expectations*. Harmondsworth: Penguin. Orig. publ. 1860/61.

Dos Passos, John (1938) *U.S.A.* New York: Modern Library.

Faulkner, William (1950) 'A Rose for Emily', in *Collected Stories of William Faulkner*. New York: Random House. Orig. publ. 1930.

—— (1965) *The Sound and the Fury*. Harmondsworth: Penguin. Orig. publ. 1931.

—— (1971) 'Barn Burning', in Warren, Robert Penn and Erskine, Albert (eds), *Short Story Masterpieces*. New York: Dell. Orig. publ. 1939.

—— (1972) *Absalom, Absalom!* New York: Vintage Books. Orig. publ. 1936.

Fielding, Henry (1962) *Joseph Andrews*. London: Dent. Orig. publ. 1742.

—— (1962) *Tom Jones*. London: Dent. Orig. publ. 1749.

Flaubert, Gustave (1965) *Madame Bovary*. New York: Norton. Orig. publ. French 1857.

—— (1970) *Sentimental Education*. Harmondsworth: Penguin. Orig. publ. in French 1869.

Forster, Edward Morgan (1963) *A Passage to India*. Harmondsworth: Penguin. Orig. publ. 1924.

Gide, André (1949) *Les faux monnayeurs (The Counterfeiters)*. Paris: Gallimard.

Hardy, Thomas (1963) *Tess of the D'Urbervilles*. London: Macmillan. Orig. publ. 1891.

Hemingway, Ernest (1965) 'The Killers' and 'Hills like White Elephants', in *Men without Women*. Harmondsworth: Penguin. Orig. publ. 1928.

James, Henry (1959) *The Sacred Fount*. London: Rupert Hart-Davis. Orig. publ. 1901.

—— (1964) 'The Figure in the Carpet', in *The Complete Tales of Henry James*. London: Rupert Hart-Davis. Orig. publ. 1896.

—— (1966) *The Portrait of a Lady*. Harmondsworth: Penguin. Orig. publ. 1881.

—— (1973) The Turn of the Screw and Other Stories. Harmondsworth: Penguin. Orig. publ. 1898.

Joyce, James (1961) 'Eveline', in *Dubliners*. Harmondsworth: Penguin. Orig. publ. 1914.

—— (1963) *A Portrait of the Artist as a Young Man*. Harmondsworth: Penguin. Orig. publ. 1916.

Kleist, Heinrich von (1962) 'The Marquise of O-', in *The Marquise of O- and Other Stories*. New York: Signet. Orig. publ. in German 1806.

Lawrence, D. H. (1961) *Lady Chatterley's Lover*. Harmondsworth: Penguin. Orig. publ. 1928.

—— (1962) *Sons and Lovers;* Harmondsworth: Penguin. Orig. publ. 1913.

—— (1973) *The Rainbow.* Harmondsworth: Penguin. Orig. publ. 1915.

Le Carré, John (1965) *The Spy Who Came in from the Cold.* New York: Dell. Orig. publ. 1963.

McCullers, Carson (1971) 'The Sojourner', in Warren, Robert Penn and Erskine, Albert (eds), *Short Story Masterpieces*. New York: Dell. Orig. publ. 1951.

Melville, Herman (1964) *Pierre, or the Ambiguities.* New York: Signet. Orig. publ. 1852.

Nabokov, Vladimir (1969) *Laughter in the Dark.* London: Weidenfeld & Nicolson. Orig. publ. in Russian 1933.

—— (1971) *The Real Life of Sebastian Knight.* Harmondsworth: Penguin. Orig. publ. 1941.

Porter, Katherine Anne (197 1) 'Flowering Judas', in Warren, Robert Penn and Erskine, Albert (eds), *Short Story Masterpieces*. New York: Dell. Orig. publ. 1930.

Proust, Marcel (1963) *Un amour de Swann.* Paris: Gallimard. Orig. publ. 1919.

Robbe-Grillet, Alain (1965) 'Jealousy', in *Two Novels by Robbe-Grillet: Jealousy and In the Labyrinth.* New York: Grove Press. Orig. publ. in French 1957.

Spark, Muriel (1971) *The Prime of Miss Jean Brodie.* Harmondsworth: Penguin. Orig. publ. 1961.

Sterne, Laurence (1967) *Tristram Shandy*. Harmondsworth: Penguin. Orig. publ. 1760.

Tolstoy, Leo (1950) *Anna Karenina*. New York: Random House. Orig. publ. in Russian 1873–6.

—— (1971) *War and peace*. London: Heinemann. Orig. publ. in Russian 1864–9.

Warren, Robert Penn and Erskine, Albert (eds) (1971) *Short Story Masterpieces*. New York: Dell.

White, Patrick (1960) *Voss*. Harmondsworth: Penguin. Orig. publ. 1957.

Woolf, Virginia (1974) *Mrs Dalloway*. Harmondsworth: Penguin. Orig. publ. 1925.

Zinoviev, Alexander (1981) *The Yawning Heights*. Harmondsworth: Penguin. Orig. publ. in Russian 1976.

THEORETICAL STUDIES

Aristotle (1951) 'Poetics', in Smith, James Harry and Parks, Edd Winfield (eds), *The Great Critics: An Anthology of Literary Criticism*. New York: Norton.

Bakhtin, Mikhail (1973) *Problems of Dostoevsky's Poetics*. Ann Arbor, Mich.: Ardis. Orig. publ. in Russian 1929.

*Bal, Mieke (1977) *Narratologie. Essais sur la signification narrative dans quatre romans modernes*. Paris: Klincksieck. Particularly important are the hierarchical tripartite distinction (fable, story, narrative ref-text) and the discussion of focalization and narration, criticizing and modifying Genette's theory (1972).

—— (1978) 'Mise en abyme et iconicité', *Littérature*, 29, 116–23.

—— (1981a) 'Notes on narrative embedding', *Poetics Today*, 2, 2, 41–60.

—— (1981b) 'The laughing mice, or: on focalization', *Poetics Today*, 2, 2, 202–10.

Bally, Charles (1912) 'Le style indirect libre en français moderne' *Germanisch-Romanisch Monatsschrift*, 4, 549–56 and 597–606.

Banfield, Ann (1973) 'Narrative style and the grammar of direct and indirect speech', *Foundations of Language*, 10, 1–39.

*—— (1978a) 'The formal coherence of represented speech and thought', *Poetics and Theory of Literature*, 3, 289–314. A linguistically oriented study of free indirect discourse and related phenomena. Banfield's hypothesis (here and elsewhere) concerning 'speakerless' sentences has influenced some narratologists in talking about 'narratorless' narratives (e.g. Chatman 1978).

—— (1978b) 'Where epistemology, style, and grammar meet literary history: the development of represented speech and thought', *New Literary History*, 9, 415–54.

—— (1981) 'Reflective and non-reflective consciousness in the language of fiction', *Poetics Today*, 2, 2, 61–76.

Bann, S. and Bowlt, J. E. (eds) (1973) *Russian Formalism*. Edinburgh: Scottish Academic Press.

Barnouw, Dagmar (1980) 'Critics in the act of reading', *Poetics Today*, 1, 4, 213–22.

Barthes, Roland (r964) *Essais Critiques*, Paris: Seuil. In English, (1972) *Critical Essays*. Evanston, Ill.: Northwestern University Press.

*—— (1966) 'Introduction à l'analyse structurale des récits', *Communications*, 8, 1–27. In English, (1977) 'Introduction to the structural analysis of narratives', in *Image-Music-Text*. London: Fontana. By now a classical example of the type of analysis practised in the early stages of French Structuralism. Particularly important is the analysis of 'story', with its distinction between 'functions' (subdivided into 'kernels' and 'catalysts') and 'indices' (subdivided into 'indices proper' and 'informants').

—— (1970) 'Elements of Semiology', in *Writing Degree Zero and Elements of Semiology*. Boston, Mass.: Beacon Press. Orig. publ. in French 1964.

*—— (1970) S/Z. Paris: Seuil. In English, (1974) S/Z. New York: Hill & Wang. Marks Barthes's transition from structural to textual analysis. Through a study of Balxac's 'Sarrasine', Barthes presents the codes underlying both the production of texts and their reading. Advocates plurality and reversibility.

Barthes, Roland, Kayser, Wolfgang, Booth, Wayne C. and Hamon, Philippe (1977) *Poétique du récit*. Paris: Seuil.

Beardsley, Monroe C. (1958) *Aesthetics: Problems in the Philosophy of Criticism*. New York: Harcourt, Brace & World.

Benveniste, Emile (1966) *Problèmes de linguistique générale*. Paris: Gallimard. In English, (1970) *Problems in General Linguistics*. Coral Gables, Florida: University of Miami Press.

Blin, Georges (1954). *Stendhal et les problèmes du roman*. Paris: Corti.

*Booth, Wayne C. (1961) *The Rhetoric of Fiction*. Chicago: The University of Chicago Press. The most systematic Anglo-American contribution to questions of point of view, types of narrators, the norms of the text, the notion of the implied author. Abounds in interesting examples from a wide range of literary works. Although Booth's moralistic stance has often been criticized and many of his theories have undergone modification, this remains a seminal book.

Bradley, A. C. (1965) *Shakespearean Tragedy*. London: Macmillan. Orig. publ. 1904.

Bremond, Claude (1964) 'Le message narratif', *Communications*, 4, 4–32.

—— (1966) 'La logique des possibles narratifs', *Communications*, 8, 60–76.

*—— (1970) 'Morphology of the French folktale', *Semiotica*, 2, 247–76. See comment under next item.

*—— (1973) *Logique du récit*. Paris: Seuil. A model for the analysis of 'story'. Inspired by Propp, Bremond divides every sequence into three functions and allows for bifurcation at every stage.

Brinker, Menachem (1980) 'Two phenomenologies of reading. Ingarden and Iser on textual indeterminacy', *Poetics Today*, 1, 4, 203–12.

Bronzwaer, W. J. M. (1970) *Tense in the Novel: An Investigation of Some Potentialities of Linguistic Criticism*. Groningen: Walters-Noordhof.

—— (1981) 'Mieke Bal's concept of focalization: a critical note', *Poetics Today*, 2, 2, 193–201.

Brooke-Rose, Christine (1980a) 'The readerhood of man', in Suleiman, Susan R. and Crosman, Inge (eds), *The Reader in the Text. Essays on Audience and Interpretation*. Princeton, NJ: Princeton University Press, 120–48.

—— (1980b) 'Round and round the Jakobson diagram: a survey', *Hebrew University Studies in Literature*, 8, 153–82.

Brooks, Cleanth (1947) *The Well Wrought Urn*. New York: Harcourt, Brace & World.

Brooks, Cleanth and Warren, Robert Penn (1959) *Understanding Fiction*. New York: Appleton-Century-Crofts. Orig. publ. 1943.

Brooks, Peter (1977) 'Freud's masterplot', *Yale French Studies*, 55/56, 280–300.

—— (1979) 'Fictions of the Wolfman: Freud and narrative understanding', *Diacritics*, 9, 72–81.

Bühler, W. ((1936) *Die 'Erlebte Rede' im englischen Roman, ihre Vorstufen und ihre Ausbildung im Werke Jane Austens*. Zürich: Max Niehans Verlag.

Chase, Cynthia (1979) 'Oedipal textuality: reading Freud's reading of Oedipus', *Diacritics*, 9, 54–68.

Chatman, Seymour (1969) 'New ways of analyzing narrative structure, with an example from Joyce's *Dubliners*', *Language and Style*, 2, 3–36.

—— (1971) (ed.) *Literary Style: A Symposium*. London and New York: Oxford University Press.

—— (1972) 'On the Formalist-Structuralist theory of character', *Journal of Literary Semantics*. 1, 57–79.

*—— (1978) *Story and Discourse*. Ithaca, New York: Cornell University Press. A synthesis of various theories of narrative in literature and film, discussing events, characters, time, point of view and narration. My own study sometimes relies on Chatman and often disagrees with him. Particularly important is the section on character, criticizing its reductive treatment by formalists and structuralists, and suggesting an analysis in terms of a paradigm of traits.

Cixous, Hélène (1974) 'The character of "character"', *New Literary History*, 5, 383–402.

Cohn, Dorrit (1966) 'Narrated monologue: definition of a fictional style', *Comparative Literature*, 28, 97–112.

—— (1978) *Transparent Minds: Narrative Modes for Presenting Consciousness in Fiction*. Princeton, NJ: Princeton University Press.

—— (1981) 'The encirclement of narrative: on Franz Stanzel's *Theorie des Erzählens*', *Poetics Today*, 2,12, 157–82.

Copi, Irving M. (1961) *Introduction to Logic*. New York: Macmillan. Orig. publ. 1953.

Courtés, Joseph (1976) *Introduction à la sémiotique narrative et discursive*. Paris: Hachette Université.

*Culler, Jonathan (1975) *Structuralist Poetics. Structuralism, Linguistics and the Study of Literature*. London: Routledge & Kegan Paul. A lucid survey of structuralist theories of both poetry and narrative, as well as a presentation of the linguistic and anthropological basis of structuralism. Argues for a poetics grounded in a theory of reading.

—— (1980) 'Fabula and Sjuzhet in the analysis of narrative. Some American discussions', *Poetics Today*, 1, 3, 27–37.

—— (1981) *The Pursuit of Signs: Semiotics, Literature, Deconstruction*. London: Routledge & Kegan Paul.

Dällenbach, Lucien (1977) *Le récit spéculaire. Essai sur la mise en abyme*. Paris: Seuil.

de Man, Paul (1971) *Blindness and Insight Essays in the Rhetoric of Contemporary Criticism*. New York: Oxford University Press.

—— (1979) *Allegories of Reading: Figural Language in Rousseau, Nietzsche, Rilke, and Proust*. New Haven, Conn.: Yale University Press

Derrida, Jacques (1967a) 'Freud et la scene de L'Ecriture', in *L'Ecriture et la différence*. Paris: Seuil.

—— (1967b) *De la grammatologie*. Paris: Minuit.

—— (1972) *Marges de la philosophie*. Paris: Minuit.

—— (1973) 'Différance', in *Speech and Phenomena and Other Essays on Husserl's Theory of Signs*. Evanston, Ill.: Northwestern University Press, pp. 129–60. Orig. publ. in French 1967.

—— (1977) 'Signature event context', *Glyph*, 1, 172–97. Orig. publ. in French 1972.

Doležel, Lubomír (1971) 'Toward a structural theory of content in prose fiction', in Chatman, Seymour (ed.), *Literary Style: A Symposium*. London and New York: Oxford University Press, 95–110.

—— (1980) 'Eco and his model reader', *Poetics Today*, 1, 4, 181–3.

Eco, Umberto (1979) *The Role of the Reader: Explorations in the Semiotics of Texts*. Bloomington and London: Indiana University Press.

Eikhenbaurn, Boris (1971) 'The theory of the formal method', in Matejka, Ladislav and Pomorska, Krystyna (eds), *Readings in Russian Poetics*. Cambridge, Mass.: The MIT Press. Orig. publ. in Russian 1925.

Erlich, Victor (1969) *Russian Formalism. History-Doctrine*. The Hague: Mouton.

Even-Zohar, Itamar (1968/9) 'Correlative positive and correlative negative time in Strindberg's *The Father* and *A Dream Play*' (in Hebrew), *Hasifrut*, 1, 538–68. English abstract pp. vi–vii.

Ewen, Joseph (1968) 'Represented speech: a concept in the theory of prose and its uses in Hebrew fiction' (in Hebrew), *Hasifrut*, 1, 140–52. English abstract pp. xi–xii.

—— (1971) 'The theory of character in narrative fiction' (in Hebrew), *Hasifrut*, 3, 1–30. English abstract pp. i–ii.

—— (1974) 'Writer, narrator, and implied author' (in Hebrew), *Hasifrut*, 18–19, 137–63. English abstract pp. vii–ix.

—— (1978) *A Dictionary of Narrative Fiction* (in Hebrew). Jerusalem: Akademon.

*—— (1980) *Character in Narrative* (in Hebrew). Tel Aviv: Sifri'at Po'alim. Grapples with the complex problem of character and presents a clear and useful analysis of various methods of characterization. Unfortunately available only in Hebrew. A brief outline in English is attached to Ewen's 1971 article.

Felman, Shoshana (1977) 'Turning the screw of interpretation', *Yale French Studies*, 55/56, 94–207.

Ferrara, Fernando (1974) 'Theory and model for the structural analysis of fiction', *New Literary History*, 5, 245–68.

Fish, Stanley E. (1970) 'Literature in the reader: affective stylistics', *New Literary History*, 2, 123–62.

*—— (1980) *Is There a Text in This Class?* Cambridge, Mass.: Harvard

University Press. A collection of early and more recent articles, dealing with the complex relations between text and reader, with an emphasis on the latter.

Forster, E. M. (1963) *Aspects of the Novel*. Harmondsworth: Penguin. Orig. publ. 1927.

Fowler, Roger (1977) *Linguistics and the Novel*. London and New York: Methuen.

Friedman, Norman (1955) 'Point of view in fiction: the development of a critical concept', *PMLA*, 70, 1160–84.

Garvey, James (1978) 'Characterization in narrative', *Poetics*, 7, 63–78.

Genette, Gérard (1969) *Figures II*. Paris: Seuil.

*—— (1972) *Figures III* Paris: Seuil. In English, (1980) *Narrative Discourse*. Ithaca, NY: Cornell University Press. A brilliant combination of theoretical and descriptive poetics, analysing both the system governing all narratives and its operation in Proust's *A la recherche du temps perdu*. Particularly new is the section on temporal frequency and the distinction between focalization and narration.

Gibson, Walker (1950) 'Authors, speakers, readers, mock readers', *College English*, 11, 265–9.

Gide, André (1948) *Journal 1889–1939*. Paris: Gallimard.

Glauser, Lisa (1948) *Die erlebte Rede im englitchen Roman des 19 Jahrhunderts*. Bern: A. Francke.

Golomb, Harai (1968) 'Combined speech – a major technique in the prose of S. Y. Agnon: its use in the story "A Different Face"' (in Hebrew), *Hasifrut*, 1, 25 1–62. English abstract pp. v–vi.

Greimas, Algirdas Julien (1966) *Sémantique structurale*. Paris: Larousse.

—— (1970) *Du Sens*. Paris: Seuil.

—— (1971) 'Narrative grammar: units and levels', *Modem Language Notes*, 86, 793–806.

*—— (1973) 'Les actants, les acteurs et les figures', in Chabrol, C. (ed.), *Sémiotique narrative et textuelle*. Paris: Larousse. An extreme structuralist view, reducing characters to their participation in the action.

*—— (1976) *Maupassant. La sémiotique du texte. Exercices pratiques*. Paris: Seuil. Developing the theories he started forming in 1966 and 1970 (see above), Greimas also applies them to a story by Maupassant, showing how the deep-structure semiotic square manifests itself at the surface structure.

—— (1977) 'Elements of a narrative grammar', *Diacritics*, 7, 23–40. Orig. publ. in French 1969.

Greimas, Algirdas Julien and Courtés, Joseph (1979) *Sémotique: un dictionnaire raisonné de la théorie du langage.* Paris: Hachette.

Groupe d'Entrevernes (1979) *Analyse sémiotique des Textes. Introduction, Théorie-Pratique.* Lyon: Presses Universitaires de Lyon.

Halperin, John (ed.) (1974) *The Theory of the Novel: New Essays.* New York: Oxford University Press.

Hamburger, Käte (1951) 'Zum Strukturproblem der epischen und dramatischen Dichtung', DV, 25, 1–25.

—— (1973) *The Logic of Literature.* Bloomington: Indiana University Press. Orig. publ. in German 1957.

*Hamon, Philippe (1977) 'Pour un statut sémiologique du personnage', in Barthes *et al.*, op. cit., pp. 117–63. Orig. publ. 1972. One of the few attempts at a systematic theory of character within a semiotic framework.

*Hawkes, Terence (1977) *Structuralism and Semiotics.* London: Methuen. A very useful introduction to structuralism and semiotics. Since this book is organized according to theoreticians, it could be read as an important companion to my own study which is organized according to issues. Excellent classified bibliography.

*Hénault, Anne (1979) *Les enjeux de la sémiotique.* Paris: Presses Universitaires de France. A clear introduction to Greimas's difficult theory. Recommended to beginners before tackling Greimas himself.

Hernadi, Paul (1971) 'Verbal worlds between action and vision: a theory of the modes of poetic discourse', *College English,* 33, 1, 18–31.

Hjelmslev, Louis (1961) *Prolegomena to a Theory of Language.* Madison, Wis.: The University of Wisconsin Press.

Hrushovski, Benjamin (1976a) *Segmentation and Motivation in the Text Continuum of Literary Prose. The First Episode of War and Peace.* Tel-Aviv: The Porter Institute for Poetics and Semiotics.

—— (1976b) 'Poetics, criticism, science: remarks on the fields and responsibilities of the study of literature', *Poetics and Theory of Literature,* 1, iii–xxxv.

—— (1979) 'The structure of semiotic objects. A three-dimensional model', *Poetics Today,* 1, 1–2, 363-76.

Hrushovski, Benjamin and Ben-Porat, Ziva (1974) *Structuralist Poetics in Israel.* Tel-Aviv: The Porter Institute for Poetics and Semiotics.

Huxley, Aldous (ed.) (1932) *The Letters of D. H. Lawrence.* London: Heinemann.

Ingarden, Roman (1973) *The Literary Work of Art: An Investigation on the Borderlines of Ontology, Logic, and Theory of Literature.* Evanston, Ill.: Northwestern University Press. Orig. publ. in Polish 1931.

Iser, Wolfgang (1971a) 'The reading process: a phenomenological approach', *New Literary History*, 3, 279–99.

—— (1971b) 'Indeterminacy and the reader's response to prose fiction', in Miller, J. Hillis (ed.), *Aspects of Narrative*. New York: Columbia University Press.

*—— (1974) *The Implied Reader: Patterns of Communication in Prose Fiction from Bunyan to Beckett*. Baltimore, Md: Johns Hopkins University Press. One of the most important contributions to the phenomenology of reading, studying both the reader's role in 'actualizing' the text and the ways in which the text guides and controls such actualization.

—— (1978) *The Act of Reading: A Theory of Aesthetic Response*. Baltimore, Md: Johns Hopkins University Press. Orig. publ. in German 1976.

Jakobson, Roman (1 960) 'Closing statement: linguistics and poetics', in Sebeok, Thomas A. (ed.), *Style in Language*. Cambridge, Mass.: The MIT Press, pp. 350–77.

James, Henry (1962) *The Art of the Novel. Critical Prefaces by Henry James*. New York and London: Charles Scribner's Sons. Orig. publ. in the New York edition of James's works 1907–9.

—— (1963) 'The art of fiction', in Shapira, Morris (ed.), *Henry James: Selected Literary Criticism*. Harmondsworth: Penguin. Orig. publ. 1884.

James, Hans Robert (1977) *Ästhetische Erfehrung und literarische Hermeneutik. Band I: Versuche im Feld der aesthetischen Erfahrung*. Munich: Fink.

Kayser, Wolfgang (1948) *Das sprachliche Kunstwerk*. Bern: A. Francke.

Kermode, Frank (1979) *The Genesis of Secrecy*. Cambridge, Mass.: Harvard University Press.

Kiparsky, P. and Anderson, S. (eds) (1973) *A Festschrift for Morris Halle*. New York: Holt, Rinehart & Winston.

Knights, L. C. (1964) 'How many children had Lady Macbeth?', in *Explorations*. New York: New York University Press, pp. 15–54. Orig. publ. 1933.

Kristeva, J., Milner, C. and Ruwet, N. (eds) (1975) *Langue, discours, société*. Paris: Seuil.

Kuroda, S. Y. (1973) 'Where epistemology, style and grammar meet: a case study from the Japanese', in Kiparsky and Anderson, op. cit.

—— (1975) 'Reflexions sur les fondements de la théorie de la narration', in Kristeva *et al.*, op. cit.

Lacan, Jacques (1966) *Ecrits I*. Paris: Points.

Lämmert, Eberhart (1955) *Bauformen des Erzählens*. Stuttgart: J. B. Metzler-sche Verlag.

*Lemon, Lee T. and Reis, Marion J. (eds) (1965) *Russian Formalist Criticism: Four Essays*. Lincoln, Neb.: University of Nebraska Press. Essays by Shklovsky, Tomashevsky and Eikhenbaum, introducing basic formalist concepts: '*fabula*' v. '*sjužet*', 'motivation', 'defamiliarization', etc.

*Lévi-Strauss, Claude (1968) *Structural Anthropology*. Garden City, New York: Doubleday Anchor Books. Orig. publ. in French 1958. Lévi-Strauss's structural analysis of myth has had a decisive influence on the development of structuralist poetics. Particularly important are chapters 2 and 11. The latter contains the well known analysis of the Oedipus myth.

Lips, Marguerite (I 926) *Le style indirect libre*. Paris: Payot.

Lipski, John M. (1976) 'From text to narrative: spanning the gap', *Poetics*, 7, 191–206.

Lubbock, Percy (1 963) *The Craft of Fiction*. New York: Viking Press. Orig. publ. 1921.

McCarthy, Mary (1961) 'Characters in fiction', *Partisan Review*, 28, 171–91.

*McHale, Brian (1978) 'Free Indirect Discourse: a survey of recent accounts', *Poetics and Theory of Literature*, 3, 249–87. A very good survey of various theories of FID, with many examples from Dos Passos's *U.S.A.*

—— (1981) 'Islands in the stream of consciousness. Dorrit Cohn's *Transparent Minds*', *Poetics Today*, 2, 2, 183–91.

Mack, M. and Gregor, I. (eds) (1968) *Imagined Worlds: Essays on Some English Novels and Novelists in Honour of J. Butt*. London: Methuen.

*Matejka, Ladislav and Pomorska, Krystyna (eds) (1971) *Readings in Russian Poetics*. Cambridge, Mass.: The MIT Press. A more extensive collection than Lemon and Reis, op. cit, and a better translation. Contains essays by Jakobson, Tomashevsky, Eikhenbaum, Tynjanov, Brik, Shklovsky and others.

Metz, Christian (1968) *Essais sur la signification au cinéma*. Paris: Klincksieck.

Meyer, Kurt Robert (1957) *Zur 'erlebte Rede' im englischen Roman des zwanzigsten Jahrhunderts*. Bern: Francke.

Miller, J. Hillis (ed) (1971) *Aspects of Narrative*. New York: Columbia University Press.

—— (1980) 'The figure in the carpet', *Poetics Today*, 1, 3, 107–18.

—— (1980/81) 'A guest in the house. Reply to Shlomith Rimmon-Kenan's reply', *Poetics Today*, 2, 1b, 189–91.

Morrissette, Bruce (1963) *Les romans de Robbe-Grillet*. Paris: Minuit.

Mudrick, Marvin (1961) 'Character and event in fiction', *Yale Review*, 50, 202–18.

Norris, Christopher (1982) *Deconstruction: Theory and Practice*. London and New York: Methuen.

Page, Norman (1972) *The Language of Jane Austen*. Oxford: Blackwell.
(1973) *Speech in the English Novel*. London: Longman.

Pascal, Roy (1962) 'Tense and the novel', *Modern Language Review*, 57, 1, 1–11.
—— (1977) *The Dual Voice: Free Indirect Speech and Its Functioning in the Nineteenth-Century European Novel*. Manchester: Manchester University Press.

Pavel, Thomas G. (1973a) 'Remarks on narrative grammars', *Poetics*, 8, 5–30.
—— (1973b) '*Plèdre*. Outline of a narrative grammar', *Language Sciences*, 23, 1–6.
—— (1976) *La syntaxe narrative des tragédies de Corneille*. Paris: Klincksieck, and Ottawa: Editions de l'Université d'Ottawa.
—— (1977) *Plot and Meaning: Explorations in Literary Theory and English Renaissance Drama*. Unpublished.
—— (1978) *Move Grammar: Explorations in Literary Semiotics* (prepublication). Toronto: Victoria University, Toronto Semiotic Circle.

Perry, Menakhem (1968a) 'The inverted poem: on a principle of semantic composition in Bialik's poems' (in Hebrew), *Hasifrut*, I, 603–31. English abstract pp. 769–68.
—— with Sternberg, Meir (1968b) 'The King through ironic eyes: the narrator's devices in the biblical story of David and Bathsheba and two excursuses on the theory of the narrative text' (in Hebrew), *Hastfrut*, I, 263–92. English abstract pp. 452–49.
—— (1969) 'Thematic structures in Bialik's poetry: the inverted poem and related kinds' (in Hebrew), *Hasifrut*, 2, 40–82. English abstract pp. 261–59.
—— (1974) 'O Rose, Thou Art Sick: devices of meaning construction in Faulkner's "A Rose for Emily"' (in Hebrew), *Siman Kri'a*, 3, 423–59.
—— (1976) *Semantic Dynamics in Poetry: The Theory of Semantic Change in the Text Continuum of a Poem* (in Hebrew). Tel-Aviv: The Porter Institute for Poetics and Semiotics.
*—— (1979) 'Literary dynamics: how the order of a text creates its meanings', *Poetics Today*, 1, 1, 35–64 and 311–61. As in the Hebrew articles listed above, Perry is interested in the impact of the order of

presentation on the reader's sense-making activity. Discusses central issues like primacy and recency effect, gaps, frames, first and second readings. Exemplifies by a detailed analysis of Faulkner's 'A Rose for Emily'.

—— (forthcoming) 'The combined discourse – several remarks about the definition of the phenomenon', *Poetics Today*. Paper presented at Synopsis 2: 'Narrative Theory and Poetics of Fiction', an international symposium held at the Porter Institute for Poetics and Semiotics, Tel-Aviv University and the Van Leer Jerusalem Foundation, June 1979.

Plato (1963) 'The Republic', in Hamilton, E. and Cairus, H. (eds), *Plato: The Collected Dialogues*. Princeton, NJ: Princeton University Press.

Pouillon, Jean (1946) *Temps et roman*. Paris: Gallimard.

Price, Martin (1968) 'The other self: thoughts about character in the novel', in Mack and Gregor, op. cit., pp. 279–99.

*Prince, Gerald (1973a) *A Grammar of Stories*. The Hague: Mouton. An important contribution to the construction of narrative grammar, including a discussion of the notion of 'minimal story' as well as of the distinction between stories and non-stories.

—— (1973b) 'Introduction à étude du narrataire', *Poétique*, 14, 178–96.

—— (1980) 'Aspects of a grammar of narrative', *Poetics Today*, 1, 3, 49–63.

*Propp, Vladimir (1968) *Morphology of the Folktale*. Austin, Texas: University of Texas Press. Orig. publ. in Russian 1928. A pioneering study of plot-structure, discerning thirty-one functions which always follow the same order. Characters are conceived of as 'roles' played in the action. Both Bremond and Greimas developed and modified Propp's model.

Ricardou, Jean (1967) *Problèmes du nouveau roman*. Paris: Seuil.

—— (1971) *Pour une théorie du nouveau roman*. Paris: Seuil.

Riffaterre, Michael (1966) 'Describing poetic structures: two approaches to Baudelaire's "les Chats"', *Yale French Studies*, 36/37, 200–42.

Rimmon, Shlomith (1973) 'Barthes's "hermeneutic code" and Henry James's literary detective: plot-composition in "The Figure in the Carpet"', *Hebrew University Studies in Literature*, 1, 183–207.

—— (1976a) 'A comprehensive theory of narrative: Genette's *Figure's III* and the Structuralist study of fiction', *Poetics and Theory of Literature*, 1, 33–62.

—— (1976b) 'Problems of voice in Vladimir Nabokov's *The Real Life of Sebastian Knight*', *Poetics and Theory of Literature*, 1, 489–512.

—— (1977) *The Concept of Ambiguity – the Example of James*. Chicago: The University of Chicago Press.

Rimmon-Kenan, Shlomith (1978) 'From reproduction to production: the status of narration in Faulkner's *Absalom, Absalom!*', *Degrés*, 16, f–f19.

—— (1980/81) 'Deconstructive reflections on deconstruction. In reply to J. Hillis Miller', *Poetics Today*, 2,1b, 185–8.

—— (1982) 'Ambiguity and narrative levels: Christine Brooke-Rose's *Thru*', *Poetics Today*, 3, 21–32.

—— (forthcoming) 'Varieties of repetitive narration, illustrated from Faulkner's *Absalom, Absalom!*' Paper presented at the Second International Semiotic Congress, Vienna, July 1979.

Robbe-Grillet, Alain (1963) *Pour un nouveau roman*. Paris: Gallimard.

Romberg, Bertil (1962) *Studies in the Narrative Technique of the First-Person Novel*. Lund: Almquist & Wiksell.

Ron, Moshe (1981) 'Free Indirect Discourse, mimetic language games and the subject of fiction', *Poetics Today*, 2, 2, 17–39.

Roudiez, Léon S. (1961/2) 'Characters and personality: the novelist's dilemma', *French Review*, 35, 553–62.

Sarraute, Nathalie (1965) *L'ère du soupçon*. Paris: Gallimard. Orig. publ. 1956.

Saussure, Ferdinand de (1960) *Course in General Linguistics*. London: Peter Owen. Orig. publ. in French 1916.

*Shklovsky, Victor (1965) 'Art as technique', in Lemon and Reis, op. cit., pp. 3–24. See comment under Lemon and Reis.

Scholes, Robert (1974) *Structuralism in Literature*. New Haven, Conn., and London: Yale University Press.

Smith, James Harry and Parks, Edd Winfield (eds) (1951) *The Great Critics: An Anthology of Literary Criticism*. New York: Norton.

Spitzer, Leo (1928) 'Zur Entstehung der sogenannten "Erlebten Rede"', GRM, 26, 327 ff.

Stanzel, Franz K. (1955) *Die typischen Erzählsituationen in roman*. Vienna: Braumüller. In English, (1971) *Narrative Situations in the Novel*. Bloomington: Indiana University Press.

—— (1964) *Typische Formen des roman*. Göttingen: Vandenhoeck & Ruprecht.

—— (1981) 'Teller-characters and reflector-characters in narrative theory', *Poetics Today*, 2, 2, 5–16. A compressed version of chapter 6 of his *Theorie des Erzählens* (1979). Göttingen: Vandenhoeck & Ruprecht, pp. 189–238.

Sternberg, Meir (1974a) 'Retardatory structure, narrative interest and the detective story' (in Hebrew), *Hasifrut*, 18/19, 164–80. English abstract pp. x–xi.

—— (1974b) 'What is exposition? An essay in temporal delimitation', in Halperin, John (ed.), *The Theory of the Novel: New Essays*. New York: Oxford University Press, pp. 25–70.

—— (1976) 'Temporal ordering, modes of expositional distribution, and three models of rhetorical control in the narrative text', *Poetics and Theory of Literature*, 1, 295–316.

*—— (1978) *Expositional Modes and Temporal Ordering in Fiction*. Baltimore, Md, and London: Johns Hopkins University Press. An important study of various aspects of time, with detailed examples from a wide range of novelists. This book includes material which previously appeared in article form in either Hebrew or English (see preceding items) .

—— (forthcoming) 'Mimesis and motivation', *Poetics Today*. Paper presented at Synopsis 2: 'Narrative Theory and Poetics of Fiction', and international symposium held at the Porter Institute for Poetics and Semiotics, Tel-Aviv University and the Van Leer Jerusalem Foundation, June 1979.

Suleiman, Susan R. and Crosman, Inge (1980) *The Reader in the Text. Essays on Audience and Interpretation*. Princeton, NJ: Princeton University Press.

Todorov, Tzvetan (ed.) (1965) *Théorie de la littérature. Textes des formalistes russes*. Paris: Seuil.

*—— (1966) Les catégories du récit littéraire', *Communications*, 8, 125–51. A representative article of the early period of French structuralism, contributing more to the study of 'story' than to that of the other aspects of narrative fiction. Exemplified by an analysis of Laclos's *Les liaisons dangereuses*.

—— (1967) *Littérature et signification*. Paris: Larousse.

—— (1969) *Grammaire du Décaméron*. The Hague: Mouton.

—— (1970) *Introduction à la littérature fantastique*. Paris: Seuil. In English, (1975) *The Fantastic: A Structural Approach*. Ithaca, NY: Cornell University Press.

—— (1973) 'Some approaches to Russian Formalism', in Bann and Bowlt, op. cit., pp. 6–19.

*—— (1977) *The Poetics of Prose*. Oxford: Blackwell. Orig. publ. in French 1971. Discusses central issues in the poetics of narrative fiction, such as narrative grammar, narrative transformations, gaps and

absences, character, 'how to read', etc. Contains an extensive analysis of the functioning of gaps in Henry James.

*Tomashevsky, Boris (1965) 'Thematics', in Lemon and Reis, op. cit., pp. 61–95. Orig. publ. in Russian 1925. See comment under Lemon and Reis.

Ullmann, Stephen (1957) 'Reported speech and internal monologue in Flaubert', in *Style in the French Novel*. Cambridge: Cambridge University Press, pp. 94–120.

*Uspensky, Boris (1973) *A Poetics of Composition*. Berkeley: University of California Press. Orig. publ. in Russian 1970. A study of point of view in fiction, with many examples, predominantly from *War and Peace*. Discusses four aspects of point of view: ideological, phraseological, psychological, spatial and temporal. Particularly interesting is the point about the way in which naming can convey point of view.

Voloshinov, Valentin N. (1973) *Marxism and the Philosophy of Language*. New York and London: Seminar Press. Orig. publ. in Russian 1930.

Warning, Rainer (ed.) (1975) *Rezeptionsästhetik. Theorie und Praxis*. Munich: Fink.

*Weinsheimer, Joel (1979) 'Theory of character: *Emma*', *Poetics Today*, 1, 1–2, 185–211. A provocative article which dissolves the notion of character by integrating it into 'textuality'.

Woolf, Virginia (1953) 'Modern fiction', in *The Common Reader*. New York: Harvest Books, pp. 150–8. Orig. publ. 1925.

Yacobi, Tamar (1981) 'Fictional reliability as a communicative problem', *Poetics Today*, 2, 2, 113–26.

ADDITIONAL REFERENCES (2002)

Bakhtin, Mikhail (1984) *Problems of Dostoevsky's Poetics*. Minneapolis: The University of Minnesota Press. Orig. publ. in Russian 1963.
—— (1981) *The Dialogic Imagination*. Austin: The University of Texas Press. Orig. publ. in Russian 1975.
Bal, Mieke (1977) *Narratologie. Essais sur la signification narrative dans quatre romans modernes*. Paris: Klincksieck.
—— (1986) *Femmes imaginaires. L'ancien testament au risque d'une narratologie critique*. Paris: A.G. Nizet.
—— (1988) *Death and Dissymmetry. The Politics of Coherence in the Book of Judges*. Chicago and London: The University of Chicago Press.
—— (1990) 'The point of narratology', *Poetics Today*, 11, 4, 727–53.
—— (1991) *Reading "Rembrandt": Beyond the Word-Image Opposition*. Cambridge and New York: Cambridge University Press.
Barthes, Roland (1970) 'To write: an intransitive verb' in Macksey, R. and Donato, E. (eds) *The Languages of Criticism and the Sciences of Man*. Baltimore, London: The Johns Hopkins University Press, pp. 134–45.
Beller, Mara (forthcoming) 'Neither modernist nor postmodernist. A third way' Publication of the Bielefeld Conference: World and Knowledge.
Bremond, Claude, Landy, Joshua, and Pavel, Thomas (1995) *Thematics. New Approaches*. Albany: State University of New York Press.

Brooke-Rose, Christine (1990) 'Whatever happened to narratology?', *Poetics Today*, 11, 2, 283–94.

Chatman, Seymour (1990) "What can we learn from contextualist narratology" Poetics Today 11, 2, 309–328.

—— (1990) *Coming to Terms: The Rhetoric of Narrative in Fiction and Film*. Ithaca: Ithaca, NY: Cornell University Press.

Cohan, Steven and Shires, Linda M. (1988) *Telling Stories: A Theoretical Analysis of Narrative Fiction*. London and New York: Routledge.

Cohn, Dorrit (1999) *The Distinction of Fiction*. Baltimore, London: The Johns Hopkins University Press, 109–131.

Darby, David (2001) 'Form and context: An essay in the history of narratology' *Poetics Today*, 22, 4, 829–852.

Diengott, Nilli (1988) 'Narratology and feminism', *Style*, 22, 42–51.

Felman, Shoshana (1977) 'Turning the screw of interpretation', *Yale French Studies*, 55/56, 94–207.

Fish, Stanley (1980) *Is There a Text in This Class? The Authority of Interpretive Communities*. Cambridge, Mass.: Harvard University Press.

Genette, Gérard (1972) *Figures III*. Paris: Seuil. In English, (1980) *Narrative Discourse*. Ithaca, NY: Cornell University Press.

Ginsburg, Ruth and Rimmon-Kenan, Shlomith (1999) 'Is there a life after death? theorizing authors and reading *Jazz*' in Herman, David (ed), *Narratologies. New Perspectives on Narrative Analysis*. Columbus, Ohio: The Ohio State University Press.

Hamon, Philippe (1972) 'Qu'est-ce qu'une description?', *Poétique*, 12, 465–85.

Herman, David (ed.) (1999) *Narratologies. New Perspectives on Narrative Analysis*. Columbia, Ohio: The Ohio State University Press.

Hrushovski, Benjamin (1976) 'Poetics, criticism, science: remarks on the fields and responsibilities of literature', *Poetics and Theory of Literature*, I, iii–xxxv.

Jakobson, Roman (1960) 'Closing statement: linguistics and poetics', in Sebeok, Thomas A. (ed), *Style in Language*. Cambridge, Mass: The MIT Press, 350–77.

Kafalenos, Emma (ed) (2001) 'Contemporary Narratology'. Special issue of *Narrative*, 9, 2.

Lanser, Susan Sniader (1986) 'Toward a feminist narratology', *Style*, 20, 1, 341–63.

—— (1988) 'Shifting the paradigm: feminism and narratology', *Style*, 22, 52–60.

—— (1992) *Fictions of Authority: Women Writers and Narrative Voice*. Ithaca: Cornell University Press.

Martin, Wallace (1986) *Recent Theories of Narrative*. Ithaca, NY: Cornell University Press.

Miller, Hillis J. (1980/81) 'A guest in the house. Reply to Shlomith Rimmon-Kenan's Reply', *Poetics Today*, 2, 1b, 189–91.

Morson, Gary Saul (1999) 'Essential narrative: Tempics and the return of process' in Herman, David (ed), *Narratologies. New Perspectives on Narrative Analysis*. Columbus, Ohio: The Ohio State University Press, 277–314.

Nünning, Ansgar (1999) 'Towards a cultural and historical narratology: a survey of diachronic approaches, concepts, and research projects' in *Anglistentag 1999 Mainz Proceedings*. Trier: Wissenschaftlicher Verlag, 345–73.

O'Neill, Patrick (1994). *Fictions of Discourse. Reading Narrative Theory*. Toronto, Buffalo, London: University of Toronto Press.

Phelan, James and Rabinowitz, Peter J. (eds) (1994) *Understanding Narrative*. Columbus, Ohio: The Ohio State University Press.

Phelan, James (1996) *Narrative as Rhetoric: Technique, Audiences, Ethics, Ideology*. Columbus, Ohio: The Ohio State University Press.

Prince, Gerald (1973). *A Grammar of Stories*. The Hague: Mouton.

Rabinowitz, Peter J. (1997) 'Truth in Fiction: A Reexamination of Audiences', Critical Inquiry, 4, 1, 121–41.

Rimmon-Kenan, Shlomith (1989) 'How the model neglects the medium: linguistics, language, and the crisis of narratology', *The Journal of Narrative Technique*, 19, 157–66.

—— (1996) *A Glance beyond Doubt: Narration, Representation, Subjectivity*. Columbus, Ohio: The Ohio State University Press.

Sollors, Werner (ed) (1993) *The Return of Thematic Criticism*. Cambridge, Mass: Harvard University Press.

Todorov, Tzvetan (1969) *Grammaire du Décaméron*. The Hague: Mouton.

STUDIES CONTAINING SURVEYS AND BIBLIOGRAPHIES OF NEW DEVELOPMENTS IN NARRATOLOGY

Cohan, Steven and Shires, Linda M. (1988) *Telling Stories: A Theoretical Analysis of Narrative Fiction*. London and New York: Routledge.

Darby, David (2001) 'Form and context: An essay in the history of narratology' *Poetics Today*, 22, 4, 829–852.

Fehn, Ann, Hoesterey, Ingeborg, and Tatar, Maria (eds) (1992) *Neverending Stories: Toward a Critical Narratology*. Princeton: Princeton University Press.

Fludernik, Monika (2000) 'Beyond structuralism in narratology: Recent developments and new horizons in narrative theory', *Anglistik: Mitteilungen des Verbandes Deutscher Anglisten* 11, 1.

Herman, David (ed.) (1999) *Narratologies. New Perspectives on Narrative Analysis.* Columbia, Ohio: The Ohio State University Press.

Jahn, Manfred and Nünning, Ansgar (1994) 'A survey of narratological models', Literatur in Wissenschaft und Unterricht, 27.4, 183–303.

Kafalenos, Emma (ed) (2001) 'Contemporary Narratology'. Special issue of *Narrative*, 9, 2.

Martin, Wallace (1986) *Recent Theories of Narrative.* Ithaca: Cornell University Press.

McHale, Brian and Ronen, Ruth (eds) (1990a) 'Narratology Revisited I'. Special issue of *Poetics Today*, 11, 1.

McHale, Brian and Ronen, Ruth (eds) (1990b) 'Narratology Revisited II'. Special issue of *Poetics Today*, 11, 4.

Nünning, Ansgar (1999) 'Towards a cultural and historical narratology: a survey of diachronic approaches, concepts, and research projects' in *Anglistentag 1999 Mainz Proceedings.* Trier: Wissenschaftlicher Verlag, 345–73.

Onega, Susana and Landa, José Angel Garcia (eds) (1996) *Narratology: An Introduction.* Longman Critical Readers. London: Longman.

O'Neill, Patrick (1994) *Fictions of Discourse. Reading Narrative Theory.* Toronto, Buffalo, London: University of Toronto Press.

Pier, John (ed) (1999) Special Issue Narratology. *GRAAT*: publications des groupes de recherches anglo-américaines de Tours.

Prince, Gerald (1995) 'Narratology', *The Cambridge History of Literary Criticism.* Vol VIII: *From Formalism to Poststructuralism.* Ed. Raman Selden. Cambridge: Cambridge University Press, 110–130.

Ryan, Marie-Laure and van Alphen, Ernst (1993) 'Narratology', *Encyclopedia of Contemporary Literary Theory.* Ed. Irena R. Makaryk. Toronto, Buffalo: The University of Toronto Press, 110–116.

INDEX